Exploring Doctrine

Langham
GLOBAL LIBRARY

This creative course material allows students to "kill two birds with one stone," in that they can study the English language and theology at the same time. I am most impressed with the fact that the language study does not go at the expense of the theological content: the discussion of the five Christian doctrines covered in the book are in no way "dumbed down" – rather, students are helped through a variety of learning activities to live up to the challenge of understanding genuine biblical truths. Likewise with the readings, rather than opting for simplified texts, the authors introduce passages from theologians such as Barth and Vanhoozer, and then equip the learners to engage with their arguments. In this way, the book delivers both food for thought and the necessary ingredients. I take my hat off to the authors for successfully achieving what I would barely have thought possible!

Zoltán Dörnyei, PhD
Professor of Psycholinguistics,
University of Nottingham, UK

Will Bankston and Cheri Pierson have done the global church another great service with this book! Students bound for theological study will find in these pages the concepts, vocabulary, and grammar that will support their continual growth in Theological English (TE). By focusing on selected doctrines (the Trinity, Christology, revelation, soteriology, and creation), they ensure that students are exposed to fundamental teachings of the Christian faith while they build up their language skills in engaging contexts.

Pierce Taylor Hibbs
Associate Director, Theological Curriculum and Instruction,
Westminster Theological Seminary, Glenside, Pennsylvania, USA

The authors' experience internationally and the reputation of the publishers may be the initial attraction of this book, but when readers start using it they will be helped by its organization, which makes it accessible to new readers of English without in any way watering down its subject.

Marilyn Lewis
Honorary Research Fellow,
The University of Auckland, New Zealand

This book is a much-needed act of service to the global church. While large quantities of biblical and theological resources are available in English, there has been a serious lack of theological English language learning materials. *Exploring Doctrine* steps into that gap and unlocks – with generous portions of church history! – the specialized English that the average international Bible college or seminary student needs to access these resources.

Bradley Baurain, PhD
Associate Professor of TESOL,
Moody Theological Seminary, Chicago, Illinois, USA
Co-Editor,
International Journal of Christianity and English Language Teaching

There has long been a dearth of quality materials to use in helping English language learners with theological English – a language that is more than usually nuanced and significant. Bankston and Pierson have made a first-rate contribution to filling this gap with this useful volume.

David Broersma, PhD
Associate Professor of TESOL and Linguistics,
Lee University, Cleveland, Tennessee, USA

Exploring Doctrine

A Theological English Curriculum

Will Bankston
and
Cheri L. Pierson

Langham
GLOBAL LIBRARY

Published 2019 by Langham Global Library
An imprint of Langham Publishing
www.langhampublishing.org

Langham Publishing and its imprints are a ministry of Langham Partnership

Langham Partnership
PO Box 296, Carlisle, Cumbria, CA3 9WZ, UK
www.langham.org

ISBNs:
978-1-78368-642-1 Print
978-1-78368-651-3 PDF

British Library Cataloguing-in-Publication Data
A catalogue record for this book is available from the British Library

ISBN: 978-1-78368-642-1

Cover & Book Design: projectluz.com

We dedicate this curriculum to students and teachers who will use it worldwide and to the glory of our Lord Jesus Christ.

CONTENTS

Acknowledgments

We wish to thank those who assisted us in this project. We owe much gratitude to the G. W. Aldeen Memorial Fund through whose assistance this book was made possible. Special thanks go to Diane Ancheril who has served as our research assistant. She spent many hours researching, editing, and formatting the text. She is earning her master's degree in TESOL in the Department of Applied Linguistics and International Education at Wheaton College Graduate School. We are also grateful to Lauren Nadolski who worked as our research assistant in the initial stages of the project and contributed to some of the content in chapter 2.

We are also grateful to Zonia Goa and her students who piloted some of the content in this text at a seminary in Southeast Asia. Her feedback assisted us in developing activities that were appropriate for intermediate level students.

We also appreciate the assistance of Greg Morrison, Associate Professor of Library Science at Wheaton College, for his advice throughout the project. We also extend our personal thanks to our families who have encouraged and supported us throughout the writing of this curriculum.

Will Bankston and Cheri Pierson

Introduction

Exploring Doctrine: A Theological English Curriculum is designed for English language learners at the intermediate level who want to grow in their understanding of the Christian faith. Many individuals find it difficult to understand the specialized variety of language that appears in theological materials written in English. As a result, the authors designed this curriculum to serve as a bridge between an intermediate English proficiency and theological English (TE).

Five doctrines are covered in the curriculum: the Trinity, Christology, revelation and Scripture, soteriology, and creation. The reading passages and learning activities contained in each chapter focus on content that students will need for their theology and Bible courses. Discipline-specific language is highlighted in each chapter, and the range of tasks engages learners in critical thinking and application.

The theological content and linguistic exercises are designed to assist students with their specific English language learning needs for Bible and theology. The content in this course is foundational for all TE students, regardless of their specific roles in ministry. Each chapter is organized in a similar manner and begins with a brief overview of the content followed by specific terminology related to the doctrine. Pre-reading, reading, and post-reading activities follow to help students comprehend and apply the content of the reading passages. Each chapter contains a specific grammar focus and concludes with a word analysis activity. The conclusion guides students to summarize one doctrine of their choice and to present it to peers in a short oral presentation.

This curriculum is designed to allow teachers some flexibility in its implementation. In addition, when activities use English Bible passages, instructors are encouraged to allow students to consult a Bible translation in their own language. The "Scope and Sequence" provides a flexible structure for both teachers and students as they work their way through each chapter.

The ultimate goal of this curriculum is to introduce students to various strategies so that they become efficient and independent learners, thus using this textbook as a guide rather than as a means to an end. We hope that as readers explore the doctrines covered in this curriculum, they will understand the purpose for which they have set out to improve their English proficiency:

to become better informed and faithful servants of Jesus Christ, our Savior and Lord.

A Message to Students

Welcome to our student readers! It is our hope that the content contained in this curriculum will familiarize you with theological vocabulary that you will encounter in theological material written in English. It is our intention to help you bridge to a broader range of English language resources for the purposes of study, research, or sermon preparation. Many of the tasks, activity types, and strategies in this curriculum have been tested by teachers and students around the world. It is our hope that you will gain confidence in your ability to read more efficiently and effectively as you work your way through this curriculum, whether with your teacher or independently.

Scope and Sequence

Themes	Primary Reading Passages/Skills	Vocabulary Terms	Grammatical Focuses
Chapter 1: The Trinity			
The doctrine of the Trinity, characteristics of God vs humans, Trinitarian heresies, biblical exegesis and the Trinity, church councils/creeds (Nicaea)	Main points, biblical exegesis, pre-reading, *Delighting in the Trinity* by Michael Reeves	Divine, doctrine/ doctrinal, eternal, exegesis/exegetical, heresy/heretical, incarnation, monotheism/ monotheistic, orthodoxy/ orthodox, polytheism/ polytheistic, the Trinity/Trinitarian	Relative clauses, counter-factual conditionals
Chapter 2: Christology			
Classic formulations, attributes of God (including communicable and incommunicable), "sending" in Christology, Augustine, Council of Chalcedon	Post-reading, word families, main ideas, pre-reading, reflecting and synthesizing, "Augustine's exegesis"	Blasphemy, Christology/ Christological, hermeneutics/ hermeneutical, incarnation	Comparisons

Chapter 3: Revelation & Scripture			
General and special revelation, concept of redemptive history, biblical theology and themes, typology and reading Scripture	Rephrasing for comprehension, identification of theme, pre-reading, main points, and supporting details, agreeing and disagreeing, "God's promise and fulfillment," *Delighting in the Trinity* by Michael Reeves	Biblical theology, fulfillment/fulfill, illumination/ illuminate, inerrancy/inerrant, inspiration/inspire, typology/typological	Complements with "that"
Chapter 4: Soteriology			
Union with Christ, the cross and the gospel, sin and salvation, God's grace, the importance of Scripture and avoiding pitfalls	Dividing ideas into paragraphs, main points of paragraphs, "sin and salvation," "two soteriological dangers," answering comprehension questions, *Delighting in the Trinity* by Michael Reeves	Atonement/atone, imputation/impute, justification/ justify, Reformer, righteousness/ righteous, salvation/ save, sanctification/ sanctify, soteriology/ soteriological, union with Christ, wrath	Discourse connectors
Chapter 5: Creation			
The triune Creator, the Creator and his creatures, the goodness of creation, the problem of sin, the goodness of work	Extensive reading, intensive reading, skimming, paraphrasing, supporting detail, *Every Good Endeavor* by Timothy Keller	Aseity, the created order, creation *ex nihilo*, the fall, immanence/ immanent, transcendence/ transcendent	Infinitives and gerunds

1

The Trinity

The Trinity is the doctrine that tells us who God is. It is the doctrine of the Christian God. Only the Christian God is triune. This is why we begin with this doctrine. To understand Christian theology, we must begin by understanding the triune God. As we will see, the other doctrines that we will study all rest on the Trinity. The Trinity is the foundation of all that we believe. Join us as we explore how the doctrine of the Trinity relates to theology, Scripture, and the history of the church.

Terms in This Chapter

Divine (adj.[1])
- To be God
- Of or from God

Doctrine (n.[2]) / Doctrinal (adj.)
- Synonym for theology
- A specific theological topic (e.g. the doctrine of the Trinity)

Eternal (adj.)
- Outside of time
- Without beginning or end

Exegesis (n.) / Exegetical (adj.)
- The practice of reading, interpreting, and understanding biblical texts

---

1. *adj.* = adjective.
2. *n.* = noun.

Heresy (n.) / Heretical (adj.)
- Theological beliefs against orthodoxy, especially regarding the main aspects of Christian doctrine

Incarnation (n.)
- The event of the Son of God becoming human by taking on a fully human nature

Monotheism (n.) / Monotheistic (adj.)
- The belief that there is only one God

Orthodoxy (n.) / Orthodox (adj.)
- True theological beliefs, especially regarding the main aspects of Christian doctrine

Polytheism (n.) / Polytheistic (adj.)
- The belief that there is more than one God

The Trinity (n.) / Trinitarian/Triune (adj.)
- The Christian God who exists as one God in three persons: the Father, the Son, and the Holy Spirit

1.1 Introduction

Discuss the following questions:

- What is an example of a *polytheistic* religion?
- Is Christianity *monotheistic* or *polytheistic*?

The doctrine of the Trinity states:

- There is one God.
- The Father, the Son, and the Holy Spirit are God.
- The Father, the Son, and the Holy Spirit are three persons.

As Christians, we worship one _____ in three _____.

Each person of the Trinity is fully God because each shares the same *divine* nature or essence. Therefore, each has all the divine attributes or characteristics.

Humanity has a beginning and an end, but the Father, the Son, and the Holy Spirit are *eternal*.

- What does *eternal* mean?

Exercise

Brainstorm with your class other characteristics that distinguish God from humanity and write them down in the following chart.

God	Humanity
God has no beginning. He is outside of time. He is eternal.	*We have a beginning. We are inside of time. We are temporal.*

1.2 The Trinity in Scripture

Warm-Up

God's one-ness and his three-ness are equally important. Describe God's one-ness and his three-ness to a partner.

In the following two sections, choose <u>one of the three</u> Bible passages and explain what it tells you about God. Feel free to read these passages in your own language.

Section 1: The One-ness of God

    a.   "Hear, O Israel: The LORD our God, the LORD is one. You shall love the LORD your God with all your heart and with all your soul and with all your might" (Deut 6:4–5).

    b.   "Therefore, as to the eating of food offered to idols, we know that 'an idol has no real existence,' and that 'there is no God but one.' For although there may be so-called gods in heaven or on earth – as indeed there are many 'gods' and many 'lords' – yet for us there is one God, the Father, from whom are all things and for whom we exist, and one Lord, Jesus Christ, through whom are all things and through whom we exist" (1 Cor 8:4–6).

c.   "There is one body and one Spirit – just as you were called to the one hope that belongs to your call – one Lord, one faith, one baptism, one God and Father of all, who is over all and through all and in all" (Eph 4:4–6).

Choose one Bible passage	What does this passage tell you about God's one-ness?

Section 2: The Three-ness of God

a.   "Go therefore and make disciples of all nations, baptizing them in the name of the Father and of the Son and of the Holy Spirit, teaching them to observe all that I have commanded you. And behold, I am with you always, to the end of the age" (Matt 28:19–20).

b.   "Now when all the people were baptized, and when Jesus also had been baptized and was praying, the heavens were opened, and the Holy Spirit descended on him in bodily form, like a dove; and a voice came from heaven, 'You are my beloved Son; with you I am well pleased'" (Luke 3:21–22).

c.   "The grace of the Lord Jesus Christ and the love of God and the fellowship of the Holy Spirit be with you all" (2 Cor 13:14).

Choose one Bible passage	What does this passage tell you about God's three-ness?

1.3 Trinitarian Heresies

One important reason to understand the doctrine of the Trinity is that this helps you identify *heresies*. A *heresy* is a belief that is against, or different from, orthodox doctrine.

The following are three heretical understandings of the Trinity:

(1) Adoptionism
- Jesus was *adopted* as the Son of God during his human life (probably at his baptism).
- Before that he was only a human being.
- God's *Logos* came to rest on him.

(2) Modalism
- God has a real one-ness, but his three-ness is only an appearance.
- The Father, the Son, and the Spirit are like masks that God puts on at different times in history.

(3) Arianism
- The Son's nature is like (but not the same as) the Father's nature.
- The Son is not eternal like the Father.
- The Son is the greatest creature in creation, but he is still a part of creation.

Exercise

Identify the following statements as either orthodox or as one of the above heresies.

(1) In contrast to the Father, there was a time when the Son did not exist. _Arianism_

(2) God's one-ness and his three-ness are equally important. _Orthodox_

(3) Now God appears to us as the Holy Spirit. _____

(4) Jesus lived such a good life that he became God's Son. _____

(5) The Father, the Son, and the Spirit all have the same divine nature. _____

(6) The Son was created and is not eternal with the Father. _____

(7) Jesus is greater than us, but he is still part of creation. _____

(8) Jesus is like God. _____

(9) God is really one person and only seems to be three distinct persons. _____

(10) There was never a time when the Son and the Spirit did not exist with the Father. _____

(11) God once showed himself as the Father and then as the Son and now as the Spirit. _____

(12) God did not become a human. A human became God. _____

1.4 Grammar Focus: Relative Clauses and Counterfactual Conditionals

Grammar Focus 1: Relative Clauses

Relative clauses are parts of sentences that give us information about the nouns or noun phrases that come before them. They begin with a relative pronoun, such as *who*, *whom*, *whose*, *which*, or *that*.

- The teacher, who is from Vietnam, speaks English well.
- The book that is about church history is on the shelf.

In these examples, the relative clauses give us information about the teacher and the book.

Exercise

Read the following paragraph from a recent book on the Trinity and underline the relative clauses.

Excerpt 1 from Michael Reeves's Delighting in the Trinity[3]

"Father," says Jesus the Son in John 17:24, "you loved *me* before the creation of the world." The eternal Son, who according to Colossians 1 is "before all things" (Col 1:17), the one through whom "all things were created" (Col 1:16), the one Hebrews 1 calls "Lord" and "God," who "laid the foundations of the earth" (Heb 1:10) – it is he who is loved by the Father before the creation of the world. The Father, then, is the Father of the eternal Son, and

---

3. An excerpt is a short passage from a text.

he finds his very identity, his Fatherhood, in loving and giving out his life and being to the Son.[4]

Write three relative clauses that could complete the following sentence:

The Son (1) _____ is Jesus Christ.

(2) _____

(3) _____

Grammar Focus 2: Counterfactual Conditionals

There are many kinds of conditional statements in English, but they all have two main parts:

- *Conditional clause*: If I don't sleep, . . .
- *Result clause*: . . . (then) I will be tired.

One kind of conditional statement is a *counterfactual conditional*. In these statements the conditional clause either (1) talks about something in the past that did not happen or (2) talks about something that is impossible (something that cannot happen).

Example of Type (1)
- If I had grown up in Germany, I would speak German.

Example of Type (2)
- If I were a bird, I would be able to fly.

Exercise

Read the two following paragraphs. In these paragraphs, we see both kinds of counterfactual conditionals. Circle the conditional clause and underline the result clause of each counterfactual conditional. Remember, sometimes the result clause will come before the conditional clause.

Excerpt 2 from Michael Reeves's Delighting in the Trinity

Now, God could not *be* love if there were nobody to love. He could not be a Father without a child. And yet it is not as if God created

---

4. Michael Reeves, *Delighting in the Trinity: An Introduction to the Christian Faith* (Downers Grove, IL: IVP Academic, 2012), 26–27 (emphasis his).

so *that* he could love someone. He *is* love, and does not need to create in order to be who he is . . . If he created us in order to be who he is, *we* would be giving *him* life.

That is why it is important to note that the Son is the *eternal Son*. There was never a time when he didn't exist. If there were, then God is a completely different sort of being. If there were once a time when the Son didn't exist, then there was once a time when the Father was not yet a Father. And if that is the case, then once upon a time God was not loving since all by himself he would have had nobody to love.[5]

Exercise

Use the content from the above paragraphs to complete the following statements with either a conditional or a result clause.

(1) If God were only one person, _____

_____.

(2) If God had created us so that he could love someone, _____

_____

_____.

(3) _____

_____, then the Father would not be the eternal Father.

Review the above section on Trinitarian heresies to complete the following result clauses:

(1) If Adoptionism were true, then the Son _____

_____

_____.

---

5. Reeves, *Delighting in the Trinity*, 26–27 (emphasis his).

(2) If Modalism were true, then the Son _____

_____

_____ .

(3) If Arianism were true, then the Son _____

_____

_____ .

1.5 Biblical Exegesis of the Trinity

Warm-Up

Using the word bank below, fill in the missing words for Philippians 2:5–8.

who   born   form   death   human   thing   cross
himself   servant   men   becoming   yours   yourselves

Have this mind among _____, which is _____ in Christ Jesus,

_____, though he was in the _____ of God, did not count

equality with God a _____ to be grasped, but emptied _____,

by taking the form of a _____, being _____ in the likeness of

_____. And being found in _____ form, he humbled himself

by _____ obedient to the point of death, even _____ on

a _____.

Discuss the following questions:
- What does this Bible passage tell us about Jesus?
- What other Bible passages say similar things about Jesus?

Exegetical Reading

Pre-Reading Question
Why is it important to read the Bible to understand the Trinity?

_____

_____

Work through the following exercise. Focus on what is the same and what is different between Jesus and the Father.

In his book *Paul and the Trinity: Persons, Relations, and the Pauline Letters*, Wesley Hill looks at how Paul describes the relationships between the persons of the Trinity. One text Hill examines is Philippians 2:6–11, a text that may have been a song of the early church. Hill explains how this text shows the Father's unique relationship to the Son and the Son's unique relationship to the Father. The rest of this reading exercise will follow Hill's argument, paying special attention to divine relationships. These unique relationships make the persons of the Trinity who they are, but they do not separate the one-ness of God.

Let us begin by looking at Philippians 2:6–8. In the space below, write each of the verses in your own language.

Chapter 2:6	
Chapter 2:7	
Chapter 2:8	

Verse 6 describes Jesus as "in the form of God." As Hill explains, "Jesus's [form] is the same as God's [form], since Jesus is said to be 'in' that [form]."[6] Whatever makes God uniquely God, Jesus has it. Therefore, being in the form of God, he is divine and not part of creation. This was Jesus's status before the incarnation, before he became human.[7] This is the Son's eternal status.

In contrast to "*being* in the form of God" in verse 6, the next verse describes the Son "becoming" or "being born" a human. This was a new status for the Son. However, this was not a loss of divinity, but a hiding of his glory. The Son did not lose anything when he became human, but added something to himself, namely humanity. He took the "form" of a servant. "Form" is the same word in verse 6. In the same way that Jesus eternally shares God's nature, he now shares our nature, too. Taking the form of a servant means to become human. Even more, Jesus is the Father's greatest servant because of his perfect obedience.

---

6. Wesley Hill, *Paul and the Trinity: Persons, Relations, and the Pauline Letters* (Grand Rapids, MI: Eerdmans, 2015), 89.

7. While some may object to using Jesus to identify the Son before the incarnation, we are simply following the lead of Paul in this passage.

Now let us look at verses 9–11. In the space below, write each of these verses in your own language.

Chapter 2:9	
Chapter 2:10	
Chapter 2:11	

In this section of the text, Jesus is again shown to be one with God. In particular, Jesus receives "the name that is above every name." Here Paul quotes from Isaiah 45:23 in which God says, "To me every knee shall bow, and every tongue shall swear allegiance." Jesus deserves the same response from his people that God does because of the name God has given him. What is this name? It is the name "Lord," which in Greek is *kyrios*. This term was used to translate YHWH, the special covenant name for God, in the Greek translation of the Old Testament. This means that Jesus is God, and if he is God, then he has always been God, since God is eternal.

Therefore, since both Jesus and the Father are God, we see that they share the same "form," the same nature, essence, or substance. However, we can distinguish them as persons because of their unique relationship to each other. We see these relationships in the unique actions of the Father toward the Son and the Son toward the Father. As Hill writes, "those very actions of sending, being sent, exalting, and being exalted are all required in order to preserve the identities of God [the Father] and Jesus . . . in the text."[8]

---

8. Hill, *Paul and the Trinity*, 109.

Exercise

Based on Philippians 2:6–11 and the above reading, complete the following charts.

What do the Father and Jesus share in common as God?

What are the unique actions of the Father?	What are the unique actions of Jesus, the Son?

1.6 The Council of Nicaea and Pro-Nicene Theology

Pre-Reading Activity

Discuss the following questions:

- What is an important event in church history?
- Who is someone from church history that you admire?

Extensive Reading

As you read the following passage, focus on the main points that the author is trying to say in each paragraph. Do not worry if you do not know every word.

Figure 1.1: Emperor
Constantinople
holds the Niceno-
Constantinopolitan
Creed of 381, along
with bishops of the
First Council of Nicaea
(public domain)

(1) The Council of Nicaea in AD 325 was the first universal church council. It was called because of the teachings of Arius, teachings that became known as Arianism. Arius taught that the Son was part of creation, that he was a creature. The council decided that Arianism was a heresy and that the Son and the Father were *homoousios*, a Greek term meaning that they had the same nature. While it would take several years for the whole church to accept the council's decisions, many theologians supported and developed its teachings right away.

(2) These theologians are often called the pro-Nicene theologians. "Pro" is a prefix that communicates agreement with or support of something. These theologians agreed with and supported the Council of Nicaea. The early church historian Lewis Ayres identifies "three central principles to identify a theology as fully pro-Nicene."[9] The first principle is a strong distinction between God's three persons and his one nature. This distinction means that if we say something about God's *one* nature, then we say it about each of the *three* persons. For instance, if we say that God is eternal, then we also say that the Father, Son, and Spirit are eternal. The second principle is that the Father's eternal generation, or begetting, of the Son does not make God two gods. He is *one* God.

(3) The third principle is that the three persons of the Trinity work together in unity. They all work together in every action. This is often called the doctrine of inseparable operations. While one human person performs one action, the three divine persons work together to perform one action. For instance, one pro-Nicene theologian, Gregory of Nyssa, says that each action, or operation, of God is "from the Father, through the Son, to the Spirit."[10] As an example, consider the act of the incarnation: the Father sends the Son to take on flesh, the Son takes the human nature into personal union with himself, and the Spirit forms the human nature and unites it with the Son.

---

9. Lewis Ayres, *Nicaea and Its Legacy: An Approach to Fourth-Century Trinitarian Theology* (Oxford: Oxford University Press, 2006), 236.

10. Gregory of Nyssa, *One Not Three Gods*, in *Christology of the Later Fathers*, Icthus Edition, ed. Edward R. Hardy (Louisville, KY: Westminster John Knox Press, 1954), 262.

(4) For Gregory of Nyssa, the doctrine of inseparable operations showed that God is not three persons and three gods. It showed that God is three persons and one God. Gregory says that because "God is One," the three persons work together to perform one action. The three divine persons have the same unified nature. Likewise, the three divine persons perform one unified action. The unity of God's action shows the unity of God's nature.

(5) This also means that we know about God because of what God does. God's actions show us who God is. We all have many ideas about God. But where have these ideas come from? Have they come from God's actions, which show us who he is, or have they come from our own minds? The right way to understand God is to make sure that our ideas about God come from his actions. This is how Gregory of Nyssa and the other pro-Nicene theologians understood God. They studied God's actions in the Bible to understand God rightly.

Identifying the Main Points

To find the main point of a passage, we have to ask, "What is the important idea that the author is trying to communicate?" Sometimes, authors make the main points easy to identify because they state them very clearly. For example, sometimes the main point will be at the beginning of a paragraph to tell you exactly what the rest of the paragraph is about. It can also come at the end of a paragraph, to make clear what the author just said. However, sometimes main points are not as easy to identify. Sometimes they are implied or need to be inferred, which means that the author does not put the main point in only one sentence, so the reader has to read the whole paragraph and find clues that can be put together to form the main idea.[11]

Exercise

Summarize the main point of each of the above paragraphs in one sentence in the following chart.

---

11. Thanks to Ty Kieser for his help with this passage.

Paragraph 1

Paragraph 2

Paragraph 3

Paragraph 4

Paragraph 5: Why is it important to understand God by his actions?

1.7 Reflection Activity

Read the hymn "Come, Thou Almighty King" and write your own verse in English or your native language. When you have finished, practice singing it with your classmates.

> Come, Thou almighty King,
> Help us Thy Name to sing, help us to praise!
> Father all glorious, o'er all victorious,
> Come and reign over us, Ancient of Days!
>
> Jesus, our Lord, arise,
> Scatter our enemies, and make them fall;
> Let Thine almighty aid our sure defense be made,
> Our souls on Thee be stayed; Lord, hear our call.
>
> Come, Thou incarnate Word,
> Gird on Thy mighty sword, our prayer attend!
> Come, and Thy people bless, and give Thy Word success,
> Spirit of holiness, on us descend!
>
> Come, holy Comforter,
> Thy sacred witness bear in this glad hour;
> Thou Who almighty art, now rule in every heart,
> And ne'er from us depart, Spirit of pow'r!
>
> To Thee, great One in Three,
> Eternal praises be, hence, evermore;
> Thy sov'reign majesty may we in glory see,
> And to eternity love and adore![12]

---

12. Attributed to Charles Wesley, pub. 1757.

1.8 Vocabulary

Fill in the chart below with the synonym[13] and antonym[14] of any vocabulary term from this chapter and then use the term in a sentence.

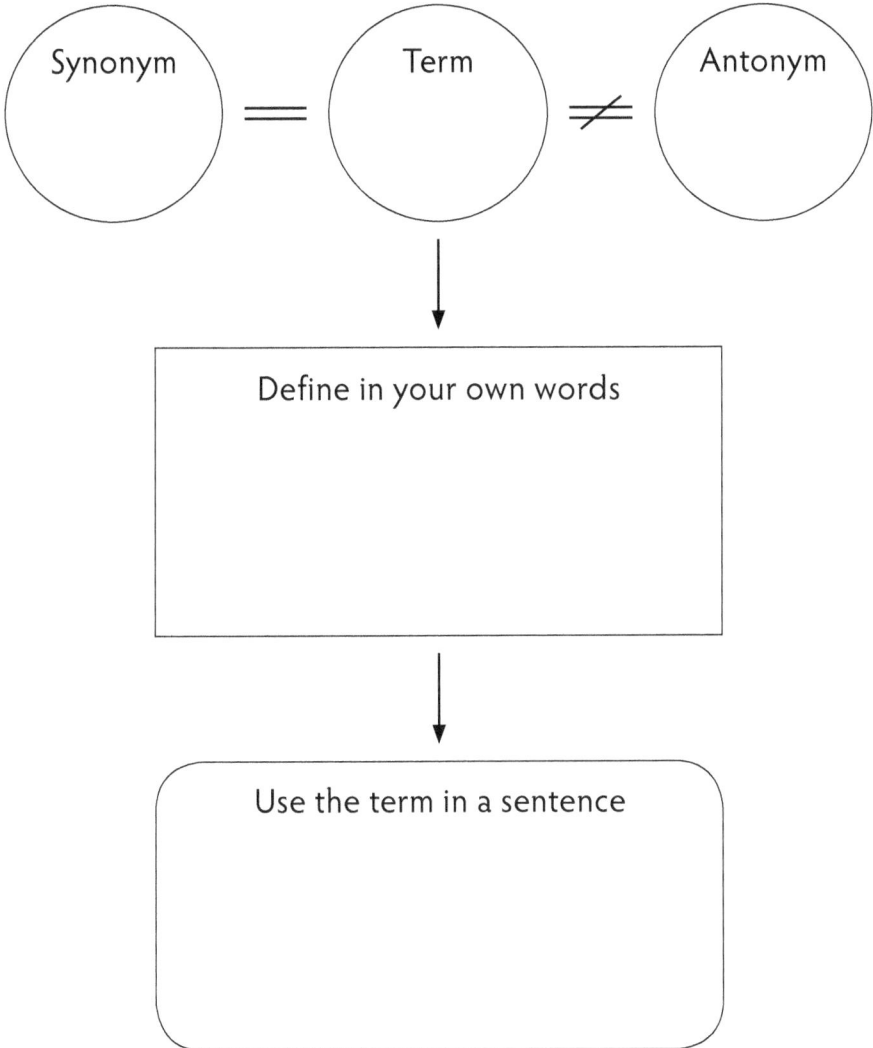

Synonym = Term ≠ Antonym

Define in your own words

Use the term in a sentence

---

13. Synonym: A word that has the same meaning or roughly the same meaning as another word.

14. Antonym: A word that has the opposite meaning of another word.

2

Christology

Christology is the doctrine of Jesus Christ. It tells us who he is and what he has done. This doctrine relates directly to the Trinity because it was the eternal Son of God who became human to save us. Christology also informs other doctrines that we will study since Jesus Christ is the one who most fully shows us who God is (revelation), the only one who can reconcile us to God (soteriology), and the one through whom God created all things (creation). Join us as we explore how the doctrine of Christ relates to theology, Scripture, and the history of the church.

Terms in This Chapter

Blasphemy (n.)
- Speech that attacks God

Christology (n.) / Christological (adj.)
- The doctrine of Jesus Christ, both who he is (his person) and what he has done (his work)

Hermeneutics (n.) / Hermeneutical (adj.)
- The study and/or practice of reading and interpreting texts

Incarnation (n.)
- The event of the Son of God becoming human by taking on a fully human nature

2.1 Introduction

Read Philippians 2:5–8, a text we looked at in the last chapter, and discuss the question that follows.

> Have this mind among yourselves, which is yours in Christ Jesus, who, though he was in the form of God, did not count equality with God a thing to be grasped, but emptied himself, by taking the form of a servant, being born in the likeness of men. And being found in human form, he humbled himself by becoming obedient to the point of death, even death on a cross.

What do you think it means to "Have this mind among yourselves, which is yours in Christ Jesus?" (Phil 2:5).

_____

_____

_____

2.2 Classic Formulations

Christ is fully God and fully human. He has a divine nature and a human nature.

However, Christ is only one person. This person is divine. This person is the eternal Son of God, the Logos.

Christ's two natures are united in his one person. The Greek term that came to be used for "person" is *hypostasis*. Therefore, we say that his two natures are united in a *hypostatic union*.

(1) The Trinity exists as _____ person(s) in _____ nature(s).

(2) Christ exists as _____ person(s) in _____ nature(s).

At the incarnation, the Son of God (who is a divine person) took on a fully human nature in addition to his divine nature.

2.3 The Attributes of God[1]

In order to understand Jesus Christ, we must understand his divine nature, the nature of God himself. This section is about God's nature and how we speak about it.

---

1. This section was taken from the work of Lauren Nadolski.

Reading

You may see a lot of new words in the reading below. Circle any words that you do not recognize, but for now do not use a dictionary.

Language is very important when forming thoughts about God. Throughout history, theologians and other Christians have studied the Bible to learn more about who God is. There are many lists of attributes, or characteristics, of God that are at the center of Christian belief.

Many of these attributes are so grand that humans do not share them. These are called *incommunicable attributes*. For example, God is omniscient, or all-knowing. This means that God knows all things, and that he knows what is happening all the time. God is also omnipresent, or present everywhere. This means that he is everywhere in the universe at the same time. God is also eternal. This means that God has always existed and will always exist. There will never be a time when God does not exist. These attributes do not describe anyone else other than God.

There are some attributes of God, however, that can be used to describe humans as well. For example, God is faithful. This means that he is trustworthy. Humans can also be trustworthy, but God is completely faithful, and will always act faithfully. Humans are not always trustworthy. God is also loving. Humans can love too, but God is all-loving. This means that he loves perfectly and is the definition of love.

There are many more attributes that are used to describe God. Many of them cannot be shared by humans, but some of them can. Some are *incommunicable* and others are *communicable*. However, when we use the same words to describe humans that we use to describe God, we are not saying that God and humanity are the same, but that humanity is reflecting what God is like.

Post-Reading
Write down one thing you learned from the reading passage. Share what you learned with your partner.

_____

_____

_____

Exercise

Now look back at the words you circled in the reading. You will see some of them below. Using the information from the surrounding context of each word, circle the best definition for each word below.

(1) Attributes
  a. people who study God
  b. characteristics or words of description (in this case of God)
  c. to have the same thing as someone else

(2) Omniscient
  a. all-knowing, or knowing everything
  b. able to live on earth
  c. kind to everyone

(3) Omnipotent
  a. readings about God
  b. very large
  c. all-powerful, or the most powerful

(4) Eternal
  a. existing forever
  b. alive for a short time
  c. an example

(5) Faithful
  a. very smart
  b. trustworthy
  c. extremely strong

Vocabulary Strategies

When we read unfamiliar words, it is easy to get confused and feel frustrated. Here are two strategies that can be used to find out the meaning of new words:

(1) Use *context clues*, or phrases around the new word, to find the meaning of the word.

Many times, the words and phrases next to the word you do not know can tell you what the new word means. Go back to the passage above and find the new words you circled. Draw a line under the words or phrases around each word that help tell you what the word means.

(2) Look for *families of words* that all have similar meanings.

Look at the following words: omniscient, omnipotent, omnipresent

What do these words have in common? _____

These words are part of a word family. In each word, *omni-* means the same thing. In theological readings, there are often words that start or end with the same parts. These words are in the same word family and can all have similar meanings. If you figure out what one of the words means, it can help you predict what the other words mean.

Practice

Using these strategies while reading a passage takes a lot of practice. You have already practiced finding out what a word means by using the context around it. Now let's practice finding out the meaning of a word from its word family. *Fill in this chart. The first word is an example.*

Word	Definition
omnipotent	All-powerful
omniscient	_____-knowing
omnipresent	_____-present

Look at the following words. Use lines to connect words that are in the same word family and fill in the chart below.

faith	grace	kind	right	truth
faithful	graceless	kindness		
graceful				
kinder	rightful	truly		
truthful	faithless	righteous		

faith	grace	kind	right	truth
faithful				
faithless				

Communicative Practice

Get into small groups. Each group will take a word from the chart above. Circle the word your group will work with. If you do not know the word, look it up in your English dictionary, and use the space below to write a definition.

Faith   Grace   Kind   Right   Truth

Definition: _____

_____

Next, find the other words that are in the same word family. Write them in the chart below. Discuss with your group what each word means. If you do not know, you can look up the word in your English dictionary. Write the definitions for each word below.

Word	Definition

Discuss the following questions as a group and write down your answers.

(1) How do these words relate to God? Is the word something God is not?

_____

_____

(2) How do these words relate to humanity?

_____

_____

After your discussion, share your answers with the class. Each group will talk about their words in front of the class. Provide the definition of each word and describe how it is or is not related to God.

2.4 The Importance of Sending

An important action in Christology is sending. Read the following Bible passages in your own language. In English, make notes of the examples of sending that you come across.

Scripture Passage	Notes on Passage
John 14:25–26	
John 15:26–27	
John 17	
Acts 1:6–8	
Acts 2:32–33	

With the help of your notes, complete the following chart on the relationships of sending.[2]

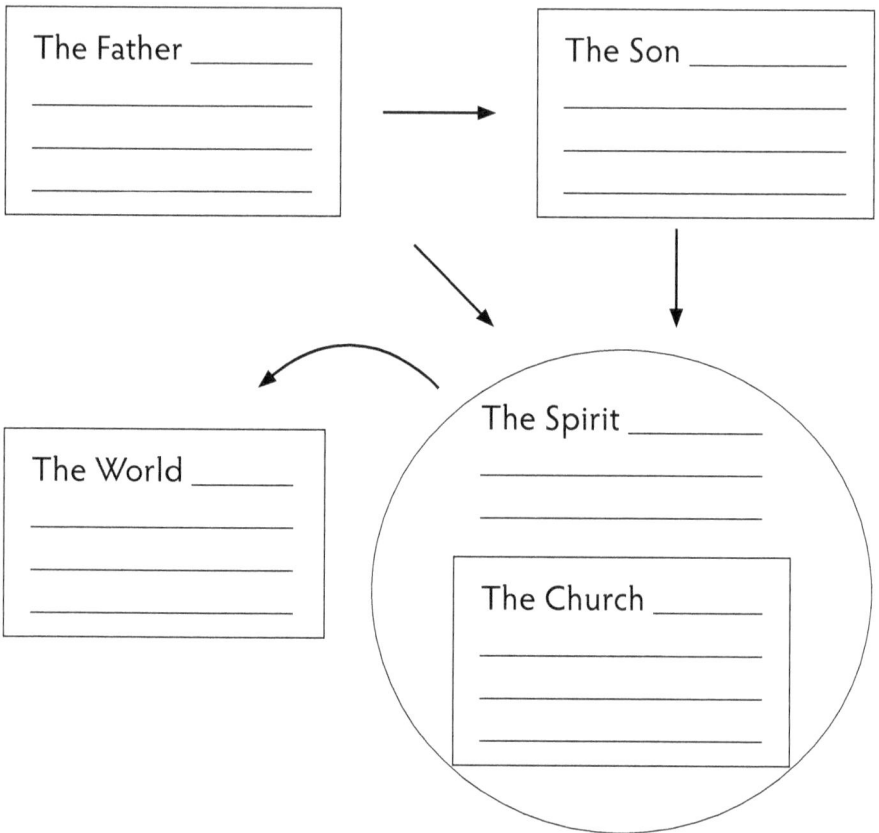

The Father _____

The Son _____

_____

The World _____

The Spirit _____

The Church _____

The acts of sending that we see in this chart help us understand the relations within the Trinity. Above we have examples of God's *economic* actions, the things God does in time for creation to achieve our salvation. These economic actions help us understand God's *immanent* actions, the things God does in eternity and only within himself. In time, the Father sends the Son, and the Spirit is sent by the Father and the Son. In eternity, the Father *begets* the Son, and the Spirit *proceeds from* the Father and the Son. As theologian Kevin

---

2. The chart has been borrowed from Cheri Pierson, Will Bankston, and Marilyn Lewis, *Exploring Parables in Luke: Integrated Skills for ESL/EFL Students of Theology* (Carlisle: Langham Global Library, 2014), 152.

Vanhoozer writes, "The way the Father and Son interact in time (i.e. the economy) corresponds to the relationship of Father and Son in eternity."[3]

Fill in the Blanks

In Time (the Economic Trinity)

- The Father _____.
- The Father and Son _____.

In Eternity (the Immanent Trinity)

- The Father _____.
- The Spirit _____.

2.5 Grammar Focus: Comparisons

Comparisons understand things in relation to each other.[4] They are used to *compare* things. One important type of comparison is an *inequality comparison*. There are two kinds of inequality comparisons: (1) "*more/-er than*" and (2) "*less than*."

(1) More/-er than

- Most (but not all) one-syllable adjectives use "-er:"
  - great – greater
  - big – bigger
  - small – smaller
  - dark – darker

  Example: Romans is <u>longer than</u> Ephesians.

- Some one-syllable adjectives have special forms:
  - good – better
  - bad – worse
  - far – farther/further

  Example: David was a better king than Saul.

---

3. Kevin J. Vanhoozer, *Faith Speaking Understanding: Performing the Drama of Doctrine* (Louisville, KY: Westminster John Knox, 2014), 75.

4. The structure and some of the examples of this section have been taken from Ron Cowan, *The Teacher's Grammar of English: A Course Book and Reference Guide* (Cambridge: Cambridge University Press, 2008), chapter 24.

- Two-syllable adjectives use both "-er" and "more":
  - "-er" (many of these words end with -y, -ly, -le, or -ow):
    - angry – angrier
    - costly – costlier
    - simple – simpler
    - narrow – narrower

    Example: Flowers are lovelier than fine clothes.

  - Most without the above endings use "more":
    - central – more central
    - certain – more certain
    - fearful – more fearful

    Example: Bethlehem is more rural than Jerusalem.

- Adjectives with more than two syllables will use "more" (with very few exceptions):
  - delicious – more delicious
  - interesting – more interesting
  - courageous – more courageous

    Example: Solomon's kingdom was more glorious than Saul's kingdom.

(2) Less than:
- This form is much simpler than the one above
- "Less" does not attach to or modify the form of the adjective
- "Less" is generally used only with adjectives of two or more syllables
  - *Saul was less faithful than David.*
  - *David was less foolish than Saul.*
  - *Saul's kingdom was less expansive than Solomon's kingdom.*

Exercise

Complete the following sentences with the correct "more/-er" form of the adjective in parenthesis.

Example: God is *more powerful* (*powerful*) than humanity.

(1) God is _____ (*wise*) than humanity.

(2) God is _____ (*strong*) than humanity.

(3) God is _____ (*faithful*) than humanity.

(4) God is _____ (*glorious*) than humanity.

(5) God's words are _____ (*dependable*) than our words.

(6) God's promises are _____ (*trustworthy*) than ours.

(7) God's works are _____ (*mighty*) than our works.

(8) God's words are _____ (*certain*) than those of humanity.

(9) God's plans are _____ (*good*) than our plans.

(10) Christ's blood is _____ (*precious*) than any other sacrifice.

(11) Christ's human birth was _____ (*humble*) than we expected.

2.6 Augustine's Exegesis

Pre-Reading Activities

Complete the two following sentences with the grammatical information above (less or more). Then skim the following paragraphs and underline each occurrence of "equal to" and "less than."

(1) Jesus's human nature is _____ powerful than his divine nature.

(2) Understanding Christ's two natures is _____ complex than understanding our one nature.

Reading

The church father Augustine gives us a hermeneutical rule for understanding both Christ's speech in Scripture and passages about him in Scripture. It is a "rule of interpretation." It states that "the Son is equal to the Father in the form of God" and "less than the Father in the form of man."[5] Therefore, when

---

5. Augustine, *The Trinity*, trans. Edmund Hill O.P., ed. John E. Rotelle O.S.A., 2nd ed. (New York: New City Press, 2012), 1.3.14.

we read an utterance of or about Jesus in Scripture, we must ask if the passage communicates according to the form of God or according to the form of man (the form of a human servant). As Augustine writes, if "we know this rule for understanding the scriptures about God's Son and can . . . distinguish . . . them, one tuned to the form of God in which he . . . is equal to the Father, the other tuned to the form of a servant which he took and is less than the Father, [then] we will not be upset by statements in the holy books that appear to [contradict] each other."[6]

Augustine explains this rule by looking at specific passages. He writes, "In the form of God the Son is equal to the Father, and so is the Holy Spirit, since neither of them is a creature . . . In the form of a servant, however, he is less than the Father, because he himself said 'The Father is greater than I' (John 14:28); he is also less than himself, because it is said of him that 'he emptied himself' (Phil 2:7); and he is less than the Holy Spirit, because he himself said, 'Whoever utters a blasphemy against the Son of man, it will be forgiven him; but whoever utters one against the Holy Spirit, it will not be forgiven him' (Matt 12:32)."[7]

Identifying the Main Ideas

All of the sentences below are true, but check only the ones that describe the main ideas of the above reading:

_____ (1) How we read the Bible is important.

_____ (2) Christ speaks in two different ways according to his two different natures.

_____ (3) We need the Bible to understand our sin.

_____ (4) Augustine had many struggles in his life.

_____ (5) When Jesus's words seem contradictory, we must know that he is both human and divine.

_____ (6) We must understand who Christ is to understand what he is saying.

_____ (7) The Holy Spirit is a person in the Trinity.

_____ (8) Reading Scripture every day is important.

---

6. Augustine, *The Trinity*, 1.3.14.
7. Augustine, 1.3.14.

Augustine goes on to offer the following examples of biblical passages. Decide whether they speak of Christ according to the form of God or humanity.

Passage	Form of God or Humanity?
"All things were made through him, and without him was not any thing made that was made" (John 1:3)	
"My soul is very sorrowful, even to death" (Matt 26:38)	
Christ came "not to do [his] own will but the will of him who sent [him]" (John 6:38)	
"I and the Father are one" (John 10:30)	
Christ was "born of woman, born under the law" (Gal 4:4)	
"For as the Father has life in himself, so he has granted the Son also to have life in himself" (John 5:26)	
"He is the true God and eternal life" (1 John 5:20)	
"He humbled himself by becoming obedient to the point of death, even death on a cross" (Phil 2:8)	
"All that the Father has is mine" (John 16:15)	

2.7 The Council of Chalcedon: Before and After

Pre-Reading Activity

Skim the article below and highlight the first occurrences of the Council of Chalcedon, the Council of Nicaea, Cyril, and Maximus. This will help you organize the main points of the article.

Reading

Now read the article and pay special attention to the main theological points of each event and person in the article. Do not worry if you do not understand every word.

The Council of Chalcedon was convened in AD 451, and it built upon the Council of Nicaea, which took place in AD 325. While Nicaea focused mainly on the doctrine of the Trinity, Chalcedon focused upon Christology. As Lewis Ayres points out, a core belief of pro-Nicene theologians was that if something belonged to the divine nature, then it was one and it belonged to the three divine persons in the same way.[8] For instance, each of the divine attributes describes the one divine nature. When we say that God is eternal, we are speaking of the divine nature that is shared by the Father, Son, and Holy Spirit. On the other hand, when we speak of "being begotten," we are speaking only of the Son. Accordingly, the distinction between person and nature became very important in understanding both the Trinity and Jesus Christ.

Before Nicaea, a controversy arose between Cyril of Alexandria (c. AD 376–444) and Nestorius regarding how many persons are in Christ. Nestorius claimed that there are two persons in Christ, a divine person and a human person. Cyril feared that this formulation meant that there were two Sons, rather than the one Son of God. He argued for the hypostatic union – that Christ's divine and human natures were united in the one divine person, who is the Son of God, the Logos himself. Furthermore, it is important to note that when Cyril speaks of a human nature, he speaks of a human body, mind, and soul. At the incarnation, when the Son of God became human, he took every part of our humanity.

Cyril's understanding of the term "person" is that of an actor, an agent. He writes, "both the manly as well as the godly sayings were uttered by one subject"[9] – that is, both the divine actions and the human actions were the actions of the one divine person. As John McGuckin writes of Cyril's Christology, there is "only one personal subject of the divine and human actions."[10] Therefore, Christ's one person acts through his two natures to produce two different kinds of actions. Eventually Cyril's theology was received as the orthodox formulation

---

8. Lewis Ayres, *Nicaea and Its Legacy: An Approach to Fourth-Century Trinitarian Theology* (Oxford: Oxford University Press, 2006), 236.

9. Cyril of Alexandria, "The Third Letter to Nestorius," in John Anthony McGuckin, *Saint Cyril of Alexandria and the Christological Controversy*, reprint ed. (Crestwood, NY: St Vladimir's Seminary Press, 2010), 271.

10. McGuckin, *Saint Cyril of Alexandria and the Christological Controversy*, 212.

at the Council of Ephesus in AD 431. Then, twenty years later, the Council of Chalcedon further distinguished Christ's one person and two natures. That is, while the Trinity exists as three persons in one nature, Christ exists as two natures in one person.

After Chalcedon, another controversy arose known as the Monothelite Controversy. Monothelite is a Greek term that means "one will." The Monothelites believed that Christ has only one will. However, Maximus the Confessor (c. AD 580–662) fought against Monothelitism and argued for Dyothelitism, a Greek term meaning "two wills." He believed that Christ has two wills. This is because Maximus understood the will to be part of one's nature and not a part of one's person. Therefore, since Jesus has two natures, he has two wills. But what exactly is a *will* in Maximus's theology? In Maximus's formulation, the will produces desires that agree with one's nature. It makes us desire certain things and we act to fulfill these desires as persons.[11] The nature produces desires through the will and the person chooses to act on these desires.

This might seem like an unimportant formulation, but Maximus uses it to understand many texts about Jesus in the Bible. For example, when John 1:43 speaks of Jesus going into Galilee, this can only be an action from the human will because God is by nature "absent from no place."[12] In "going" he was acting on a desire from his human will. The divine will cannot desire to go to a particular place because the divine nature is omnipresent. The divine nature is already in every place. Similarly, when Jesus says, "I thirst," on the cross (John 19:28),[13] or when he speaks of his wish to eat the Passover meal with his disciples (Luke 22:15),[14] he is communicating the desires of his human nature. Only the human nature in Christ, and not the divine nature, desires food and drink. However, in Matthew 23:37 and Luke 13:34, Jesus communicates his desire to gather the people of Jerusalem as a hen gathers her chicks. Maximus points out that this desire is divine because (1) it describes God's desire to be with his people, and (2) this desire is older than the human nature of Jesus.[15] This supports Chalcedonian orthodoxy and helps us better understand how Christ's one divine person acts through his two natures.

---

11. Ian McFarland, "Theology of the Will," in *The Oxford Handbook of Maximus the Confessor*, ed. Pauline Allen and Bronwen Neil (New York: Oxford University Press, 2015), 521.

12. Maximus the Confessor, *Disputations with Pyrrhus*, trans. Joseph P. Farrell (Waymart, PA: St. Tikhon's Monastery Press, 2014), 95.

13. Maximus, *Disputations with Pyrrhus*, 95.

14. Maximus, 97.

15. Maximus, 100.

Putting It Together

Write down one important theological point for each event or person in the circles below.

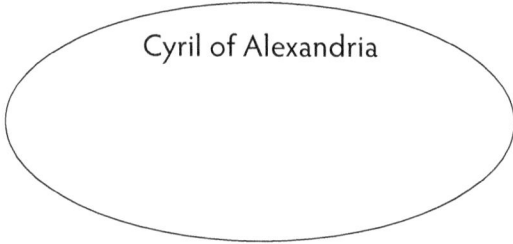

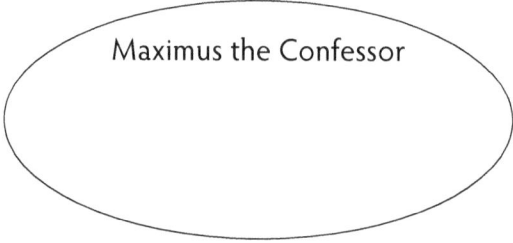

The Council of Nicaea

Cyril of Alexandria

The Council of Chalcedon

Maximus the Confessor

Define person and nature in your own words:

Person: _____

_____

Nature: _____

_____

Reflection

Look again at the earlier article on Augustine's exegesis. Identify two similarities between the exegesis of Augustine and that of Maximus.

(1) _____

_____

(2) _____

_____

2.8 Vocabulary

Choose a vocabulary term from this chapter and fill in the following boxes:

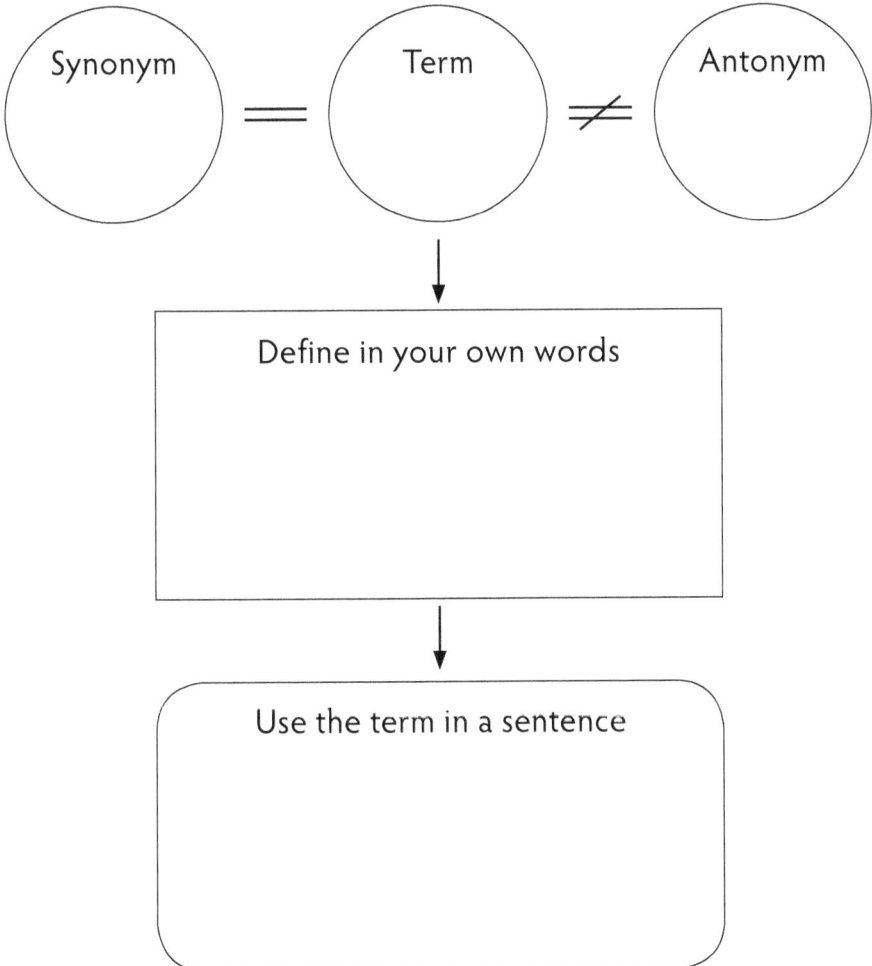

Synonym $=$ Term $\neq$ Antonym

Define in your own words

Use the term in a sentence

3

Revelation and Scripture

The doctrine of revelation tells us about how and why God communicates himself to humans. It is by revelation alone that we know who God is and what he has done. However, as we will see, it is only through a particular kind of revelation that we know God to be triune and to be our savior. Join us as we explore how the doctrine of revelation relates to theology, Scripture, and the history of the church.

Terms in This Chapter

Biblical theology (noun phrase[1])
- A theological method that follows biblical themes in Scripture through the course of redemptive history

Fulfillment (n.) / Fulfill (v.[2])
- In the Bible, this speaks of God doing what he promised to do

Illumination (n.) / Illuminate (v.)
- The process by which the Holy Spirit enables Christians to understand, believe, and love what they read in Scripture

Inerrancy (n.) / Inerrant (adj.)
- The doctrine that states that Scripture is true and without error in everything it affirms

Inspiration (n.) / Inspire (v.)
- The process by which the Holy Spirit worked through the human writers of Scripture to produce texts that are authored fully by God and fully by humans

---

1. Noun phrase: a word or group of words that functions in a sentence as subject, object, or prepositional object.

2. *v.* = verb.

Typology (n.) / Typological (adj.)
- A hermeneutical practice that interprets Christ as the perfection of important roles and institutions found in the Old Testament

3.1 Two Kinds of Revelation

Revelation is how we know about God. Revelation is God's communication of himself to humans. God has revealed himself in two ways: (1) general revelation and (2) special revelation. Everything in creation is general revelation, but only the Bible is special revelation.

(1) General Revelation: Creation

General revelation does two main things.
- First, general revelation gives us knowledge of God as creator. It shows us his care for his creatures and his wisdom in the many things he has created. However, it does not give us knowledge of God as Trinity or as our savior. General revelation does not give us the knowledge of Christ we need for salvation.
  - Psalms 19:1–2 tells us, "The heavens declare the glory of God, and the sky above proclaims his handiwork. Day to day pours out speech, and night to night reveals knowledge."
  - Think of some part of creation that you love (perhaps the ocean, stars, food, rain, trees, animals, or flowers). What does this thing that God created tell you about him?

    _____

    _____

- Second, general revelation makes us guilty before God. Creation makes it clear that there is a creator. It tells us that God exists. However, without Christ, we do not acknowledge this truth. We deny it and live as if God does not exist. Therefore, we are all guilty before God.
  - Romans 1:18–20 tells us, "For the wrath of God is revealed from heaven against all ungodliness and unrighteousness of men, who by their unrighteousness suppress the truth. For what can be known about God is plain to them, because God has shown it to them. For his invisible attributes, namely, his eternal power and divine nature, have been clearly perceived, ever since the

creation of the world, in the things that have been made. So they are without excuse."

- Why do you think people deny the truth of God that they see in creation?

_____

_____

(2) Special Revelation: Scripture

The special revelation of Scripture provides us with the revelation that we need for salvation. It is through Scripture that we know God as both Trinity (Father, Son, and Spirit) and as our savior and redeemer.

The Holy Spirit *inspired* Scripture. This happened in the past. The Holy Spirit worked through the human authors of the Bible so that both God and humans are fully the authors of the Bible. Therefore, the Bible is inspired.

- The Bible tells us that "men spoke from God as they were carried along by the Holy Spirit" (2 Pet 1:21). It also tells us that "All Scripture is *breathed out by God* . . ." (2 Tim 3:16, emphasis added).

The Holy Spirit *illuminates* Scripture. This happens in the present. The Holy Spirit works in the hearts and minds of Christians as they read the Bible. He gives them understanding of and love for the things the Bible tells us.

- Jesus tells us that "the Helper, the Holy Spirit, whom the Father will send in my name, he will teach you all things and bring to your remembrance all that I have said to you" (John 14:26). Jesus also says, "But when the Helper comes, . . . the Spirit of truth, . . . he will bear witness about me" (John 15:26).

Compare and contrast inspiration and illumination in the chart below.

List differences between inspiration and illumination	List similarities between inspiration and illumination

We can trust the Bible because it is *inerrant*. This means that the Bible is true in everything that it affirms. However, this also means that we must work hard as interpreters to understand what the Bible affirms and what it does not.

3.2 Redemptive History

Scripture follows redemptive history, which is the history of God's actions with humanity. Redemptive history has four distinct parts.

(1) *Creation:* God creates a good world without sin. God and all of creation exist in perfect relationship together.

(2) *Fall:* Adam and Eve disobey God, and they bring sin into the world. The perfect relationship between God and humanity is broken.

(3) *Redemption:* Immediately after the fall, God begins his work of redemption by promising Adam and Eve that one of their future offspring will defeat the devil. This offspring is Jesus. The rest of the Old Testament prepares the way for Jesus and his work to save God's people. This is the part of redemptive history that we are in now. Jesus has saved us, and sin has been defeated. However, sin is not yet destroyed. God's relationship with humanity has been restored, but we still wait for this relationship to be perfected.

(4) *Consummation:* When Jesus returns, he will destroy the devil and the sin that infects us. He will judge all the enemies of God, and he will live forever with the children of God. God and humanity will be in perfect relationship together, and we will never sin again.

Scripture tells us the history of God's actions with his people from creation to consummation. Below, trace the four parts of redemptive history through Scripture, starting with Genesis 1 and ending with Revelation 22. The first answer has been provided. Afterwards, compare your answers with those of your classmates.

Phase of Redemptive History	Section of the Bible
Creation	*Genesis 1–2*
Fall	
Redemption	
Consummation	

The pattern of redemptive history is *promise* and *fulfillment*. First God makes a promise and then he fulfills it. Ultimately, God fulfills his promises in the person and work of Jesus Christ.

Read the following article about how God fulfills a promise he made to Adam and Eve.

God's Promise and Fulfillment

After Adam and Eve disobeyed God, God did two things in one action. God said to the devil, "I will put enmity between you and the woman, and between your offspring and her offspring; he shall bruise your head, and you shall bruise his heel" (Gen 3:15). This promise of "bruising" is a curse of defeat on the serpent and a promise of hope to Adam and Eve. Or, as one writer says, "The deliverance of God's people always comes through the destruction of God's enemies."[3] God's people are saved when God's enemies are defeated. God promised that the devil will be destroyed and that God's people will be saved. But who is this offspring who will curse the devil and bless God's people? Who is the one who will fulfill this promise? He is the one who will represent all of God's people as their head.[4] However, his heel will be bruised. He will be wounded by Satan.

The Bible says that this promise of cursing the serpent and blessing humanity was fulfilled in Jesus Christ. He is the one who was bruised by the devil. The Old Testament tells us that the promised one will suffer. For instance, consider Isaiah 52–53. However, people did not understand the importance of suffering in the ministry of the Messiah, the Christ. For example, in Matthew 16, after Peter has rightly identified Jesus as the Christ, Peter then rebukes Jesus when Jesus speaks of his coming death (16:22). At that time, Peter could not understand that the Christ would be bruised and would suffer.

However, Jesus's "suffering is the means by which God will restore his people."[5] We are saved through the wounding of Christ. When Christ suffered on the cross, he "disarmed the rulers and authorities and put them to open shame, by triumphing over them" (Col 2:15). Like Peter, the demonic powers did not understand how Christ would fulfill God's promise. When Jesus Christ died on the cross, Satan believed that he had defeated Jesus. But the cross was

---

3. O. Palmer Robertson, *The Christ of the Covenants* (Phillipsburg, NJ: P&R, 1981), 102.

4. Geerhardus Vos, *Biblical Theology: Old and New Testaments*, new ed. (Edinburgh: Banner of Truth, 1975), 43.

5. G. K. Beale and Benjamin Gladd, *Hidden but Now Revealed: A Biblical Theology of Mystery* (Downers Grove, IL: IVP Academic, 2014), 142.

actually the defeat of Satan. The church too is a part of the bruising of the devil. Paul promises the church, "The God of peace will soon crush Satan under your feet" (Rom 16:20).

Describe the promise made by God to Adam and Eve in one sentence.

_____

_____

_____

Describe the fulfillment of this promise in one sentence.

_____

_____

_____

Choose two of the following pairs of passages. Feel free to use a Bible translation in your own language. In your own words, rephrase the first passage as a promise and the second passage as the fulfillment of that promise. Use the charts below to complete this exercise. An example has been provided.

(1) Promise: Genesis 12:3 – Fulfillment: Galatians 3:7–9

> I will bless those who bless you, and him who dishonors you I will curse, and in you all the families of the earth shall be blessed. (Gen 12:3)[6]

> Know then that it is those of faith who are the sons of Abraham. And the Scripture, foreseeing that God would justify the Gentiles by faith, preached the gospel beforehand to Abraham, saying, "In you shall all the nations be blessed." So then, those who are of faith are blessed along with Abraham, the man of faith. (Gal 3:7–9)

(2) Promise: Genesis 15:5–6 – Fulfillment: Revelation 5:9–10

> And he brought him outside and said, "Look toward heaven, and number the stars, if you are able to number them." Then he said to him, "So shall your offspring be." And he believed the LORD, and he counted it to him as righteousness. (Gen 15:5–6)

---

6. In each of these Old Testament passages God is speaking to Abram. In Genesis 17, Abram's name changes to Abraham as a result of the covenant God makes with him.

And they sang a new song, saying, "Worthy are you to take the scroll and to open its seals, for you were slain, and by your blood you ransomed people for God from every tribe and language and people and nation, and you have made them a kingdom and priests to our God, and they shall reign on the earth." (Rev 5:9–10)

(3) Promise: Genesis 15:18–21 – Fulfillment: Revelation 11:15

On that day the LORD made a covenant with Abram, saying, "To your offspring I give this land, from the river of Egypt to the great river, the river Euphrates, the land of the Kenites, the Kenizzites, the Kadmonites, the Hittites, the Perizzites, the Rephaim, the Amorites, the Canaanites, the Girgashites and the Jebusites." (Gen 15:18–21)

Then the seventh angel blew his trumpet, and there were loud voices in heaven, saying, "The kingdom of the world has become the kingdom of our Lord and of his Christ, and he shall reign forever and ever." (Rev 11:15)

Example

Old Testament Promise	New Testament Fulfillment
Passage: Genesis 12:3	Passage: Galatians 3:7–9
In this verse, God promises Abraham that people from all the nations will be blessed through him.	*In this passage Paul says that the promise given to Abraham is fulfilled in the justification of all who have faith in Jesus Christ.*

Chart 1

Old Testament Promise	New Testament Fulfillment
Passage:	Passage:

Chart 2

Old Testament Promise	New Testament Fulfillment
Passage:	Passage:

3.3 Grammar Focus: Complements with "That"

Complements are a kind of noun clause.[7] Often complements begin with the word "that." When this happens, *that* is acting as a *complementizer* and it turns the phrase after it into a noun clause. Complements beginning with *that* can act as either the subject or the object of a sentence, but it is more common for them to act as the object.

If a "*that* complement" acts as the subject, it is often followed by a form of the verb *to be*:

- That the Bible has no errors *is* amazing.

If a "*that* complement" acts as the object, it often follows verbs that describe speech, perception, or judgment:

- Scripture *says* that Jesus is both fully God and fully human.
- Paul *saw* that Jesus fulfilled God's promises in Scripture.
- The disciples *understood* that Jesus was God.
- Many people *thought* that Jesus was only a human.
- Christians *believe* that the Holy Spirit wrote the Bible.

Scan for Complements

Go back and scan the article "God's Promise and Fulfillment" and underline all of the "that complements" you find in the text.

---

7. A noun clause is a group of words that acts as a noun. For example: The Bible says *that God is the creator of the universe.*

Using Complements

Choose five of the words from the following word bank to write five sentences with a "that complement" acting as the object of the sentence. Then compare your answers with those of a partner.

say	proclaim	think	know	see
understand	find	testify	promise	believe

(1) _____

_____

(2) _____

_____

(3) _____

_____

(4) _____

_____

(5) _____

_____

3.4 Biblical Theology

Biblical theology traces themes through Scripture by following the course of redemptive history, and it shows how these themes are fulfilled in Jesus Christ. The following are some popular themes of biblical theology:

- Prophet
- Priest
- King
- Kingdom
- Rest
- Covenant
- Land
- Creation
- Sacrifice
- Resurrection

A Biblical Theology of Sonship

In the chart below, there are some passages from both the Old Testament and the New Testament that help to trace a biblical theology of sonship, specifically the theme of the Son of God. Fill in the missing boxes to provide a biblical theology of this theme.

Scripture Passage	Biblical Theological Interpretation
"I will put enmity between you and the woman, and between your offspring and her offspring; he shall bruise your head, and you shall bruise his heel" (Gen 3:15).	*God promises Adam and Eve that one day a son will be born to their family who will defeat the devil. This also means that their family will continue even though sin has brought death into the world.*
"When your days are fulfilled and you [speaking to David] lie down with your fathers, I will raise up your offspring after you, who shall come from your body, and I will establish his kingdom. He shall build a house for my name, and I will establish the throne of his kingdom forever. I will be to him a father, and he shall be to me a son" (2 Sam 7:12–14).	*God promises that one of David's sons in the future will be a king forever. God will be his father and he will be God's son.*
"For to us a child is born, to us a son is given; and the government shall be upon his shoulder, and his name shall be called Wonderful Counselor, Mighty God, Everlasting Father, Prince of Peace" (Isa 9:6).	
". . . and the Holy Spirit descended on him in bodily form, like a dove; and a voice came from heaven, 'You are my beloved Son; with you I am well pleased'" (Luke 3:22).	*Jesus is identified as the Son of God. He is the one who will defeat the devil and the one who will be a king forever.*

"But Jesus answered them, 'My Father is working until now, and I am working.' This was why the Jews were seeking all the more to kill him, because not only was he breaking the Sabbath, but he was even calling God his own Father, making himself equal with God" (John 5:17–18).	
"For all who are led by the Spirit of God are sons of God. For you did not receive the spirit of slavery to fall back into fear, but you have received the Spirit of adoption as sons, by whom we cry, 'Abba! Father!' The Spirit himself bears witness with our spirit that we are children of God, and if children, then heirs – heirs of God and fellow heirs with Christ" (Rom 8:14–17).	*Not only is Christ the Son of God, but the Holy Spirit unites us to Christ and allows the church to share in Christ's Sonship. Each member of the church, both men and women, are children of God.*
"The one who conquers will have this heritage, and I will be his God and he will be my son" (Rev 21:7).	

Tracing Your Own Theme

Now choose your own biblical theology theme. Trace it through the Bible with three verses from the Old Testament and three verses from the New Testament. Then provide an interpretation of each text.

Theme	Interpretation
OT Text:	
OT Text:	

Theme	Interpretation
OT Text:	
NT Text:	
NT Text:	
NT Text:	

3.5 Typology and Reading Scripture

Typology interprets Christ as the perfection of certain roles and institutions that we find in the Old Testament. Theologian Kevin Vanhoozer explains this practice, writing, "The New Testament as a whole employs a diversity of types that, taken together, virtually recapitulates the whole of the Old Testament: Jesus is the second Adam, a prophet greater than Moses, a priest of the order of Melchizedek, a Davidic king."[8] That is, the person and work of Jesus show him to be the perfect human, the perfect prophet, the perfect priest, and the perfect king. These Old Testament categories point to Christ and also help us to understand him. Therefore, typology helps us to see how the whole Bible is about Jesus. The reading below will help us to understand how typology affects reading the Bible.

---

8. Kevin J. Vanhoozer, *The Drama of Doctrine: A Canonical-Linguistic Approach to Christian Theology* (Louisville, KY: Westminster John Knox Press, 2005), 222.

Pre-Reading Questions

Work with a partner to answer the following questions.

Explain how Christ fulfills another Old Testament role or institution (such as the temple or sacrificial system).

_____

_____

_____

The following passage does not use the word "typology." However, skim the passage and identify which paragraph speaks of Christ's typological roles. Write your answer below.

_____

_____

Think about the question: *Why do you read the Bible?* How would you answer this question?

_____

_____

_____

Pre-Reading Activity

Scan the following passage and underline each "that complement."

Reading

The following passage is about typology and the purpose of reading the Bible. Do not worry if you do not understand every word. Focus on the main points of each paragraph.

Excerpt from Michael Reeves's Delighting in the Trinity

(1) . . . the point of all the Scriptures is to make Christ known. As the Son makes his Father known, so the Spirit-breathed Scriptures make the Son known. Paul wrote to Timothy of how "from infancy you have known the holy Scriptures, which are able to make you wise for salvation through faith in Christ Jesus" (2 Tim 3:15). He is referring to the Old Testament, of course, but the same could be said of the New. Similarly, Jesus said to the Jews of his day: "You

diligently study the Scriptures because you think that by them you possess eternal life. These are the Scriptures that testify about me, yet you refuse to come to me to have life . . . If you believed Moses, you would believe me, for he wrote about me" (John 5:39–40, 46). Clearly, Jesus believed that it is quite possible to study the Scriptures diligently and entirely miss their point, which is to proclaim him so that readers might come to him for life.

(2) It all dramatically affects why we open the Bible. We can open our Bibles for all sorts of odd reasons – as a religious duty, an attempt to earn God's favor, or thinking that it serves as a moral self-help guide, a manual of handy tips for effective religious lives. That idea is actually one main reason so many feel discouraged in their Bible-reading. Hoping to find quick lessons for how they should spend today, people find instead a genealogy, or a list of various sacrifices. And how could page after page of histories, descriptions of the temple, instructions to priests, affect how I rest, work and pray today?

(3) But when you see that Christ is the subject of all the Scriptures, that he is the Word, the Lord, the Son who reveals his Father, the promised Hope, the true Temple, the true Sacrifice, the great High Priest, the ultimate King, then you can read, not so much asking, "What does this mean for me, right now?" but "What do I learn here of Christ?" Knowing that the Bible is about him and not me means that, instead of reading the Bible obsessing about me, I can gaze on him. And as through the pages you get caught up in the wonder of his story, you find your heart strangely pounding for him in a way you never would have if you had treated the Bible as a book about you.[9]

Use the charts below to identity the main point of each paragraph and two supporting details of each main point. Some examples have been provided.

---

9. Michael Reeves, *Delighting in the Trinity: An Introduction to the Christian Faith* (Downers Grove, IL: IVP Academic, 2012), 82–83. What appears above as the first paragraph appears as two paragraphs in Reeves's text.

First Paragraph

Main Point
While many misunderstand the Bible, its true purpose is to reveal Jesus Christ to us through the work of the Holy Spirit.

Supporting Detail	Supporting Detail
The role of the Holy Spirit is to make Christ known and the Bible is the tool that the Holy Spirit uses to do this.	

Second Paragraph

Main Point

Supporting Detail	Supporting Detail

Third Paragraph

Main Point

Supporting Detail	Supporting Detail

Interacting with the Reading

Answer the questions in the following chart.

Do you agree with Reeves regarding the purpose of Scripture? Yes or No (Circle one)		
Why do you agree or disagree?		
Give three supporting details for your position.		
Supporting Detail 1:	Supporting Detail 2:	Supporting Detail 3:

Use your answers in the chart to write a short paragraph about your agreement or disagreement with Reeves. Afterwards, share your paragraph with your classmates.

_____

_____

_____

_____

_____

_____

_____

_____

3.6 Vocabulary

Choose a vocabulary term from this chapter and fill in the boxes below.

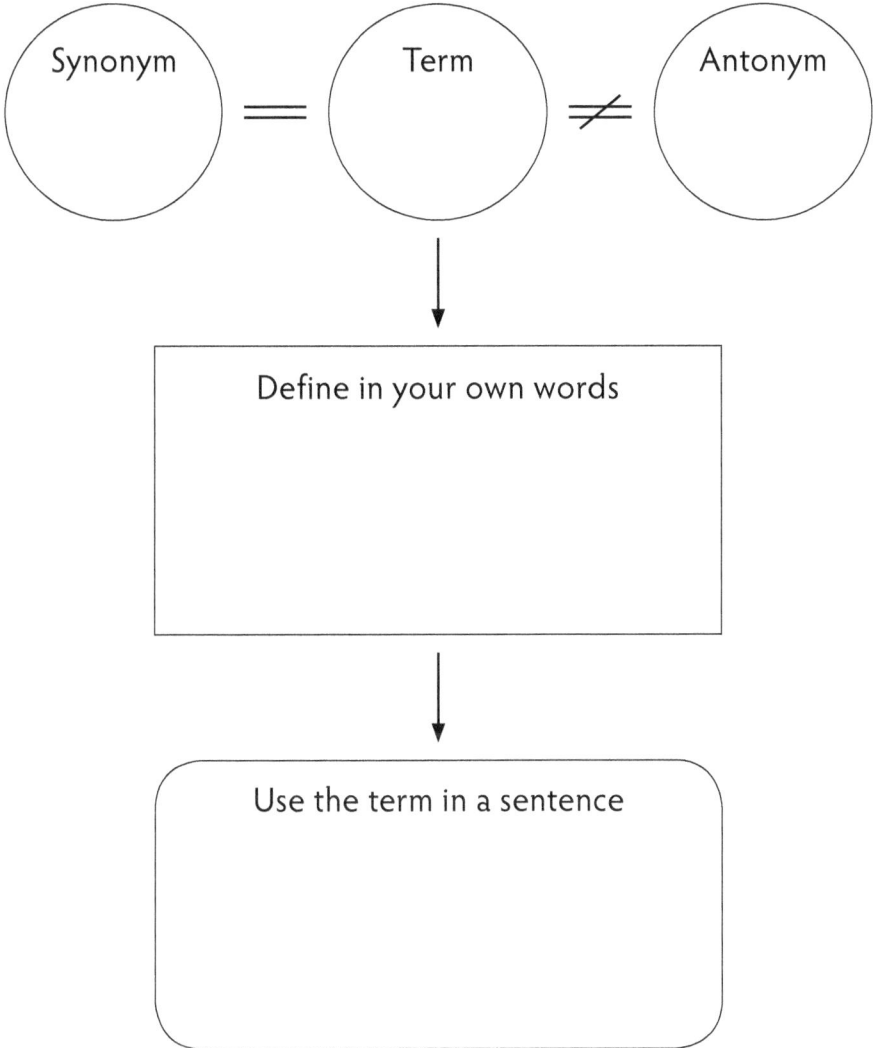

Synonym = Term ≠ Antonym

Define in your own words

Use the term in a sentence

4

Soteriology

Soteriology is the doctrine of salvation. It tells us about what God has done in Jesus Christ to reconcile sinners like us to himself. It tells us how the Holy Spirit unites us to Christ by faith and how we share in the love and life of the Trinity. It shows us the sin we have and what God has done, is doing, and will do to defeat and destroy sin. Join us as we explore how the doctrine of soteriology relates to theology, Scripture, and the history of the church.

Terms in This Chapter

Atonement (n.) / Atone (v.)
- Christ's reconciliation of sinners to God which Christ achieves by his completed work

Imputation (n.) / Impute (v.)
- General use: the act of crediting or transferring something to another person
- Theological use: the act by which Christ gives us his righteousness

Justification (n.) / Justify (v.)
- The act of God declaring us righteous because Christ has given us his own righteousness

Reformer (n.)
- A Protestant church leader during the time of the Reformation

Righteousness (n.) / Righteous (adj.)
- A right standing or status before God and a right relationship with him

Sanctification (n.) / Sanctify (v.)
- The process by which the Holy Spirit removes the corruption of sin

Soteriology (n.) / Soteriological (adj.)
- The doctrine of salvation

Union with Christ (noun phrase)
- The largest category of our salvation because all of the benefits of salvation come from this personal union
- The bond that unites us to Christ through faith by the work of the Holy Spirit

Wrath (n.)
- God's anger against and punishment of sin

4.1 Introduction: Good News and Good Advice[1]

Answer the following questions in full sentences.

What is some good advice you received recently?

_____

_____

What is some good news you received recently?

_____

_____

_____

Is the gospel good news or good advice? Why?

_____

_____

_____

The gospel is the good news of what Jesus Christ has done for us. What exactly has he done?

_____

_____

_____

---

1. Good advice is a helpful suggestion you could consider. Good news is information about something beneficial that has already happened.

4.2 The Gospel and the Cross

Read the sentences below. They are in the correct order, but they are not divided into paragraphs. In the chart below, correctly put the sentences into paragraphs. An example has been provided.

(1) The gospel is what God has done in the life, death, and resurrection of Jesus Christ to save us, to reconcile us to himself.

(2) The gospel is the good news of a completed action.

(3) It is the good news of what God has done for us in Christ.

(4) Timothy Keller points out that the gospel gives us both offense and hope.

(5) As Keller explains, the gospel tells us that "we are more sinful and flawed in ourselves than we ever dared believe."[2]

(6) This is the offense of the gospel.

(7) We are so lost in sin that only the death of Christ can pay our penalty and rescue us.

(8) And "yet at the very same time," says Keller, the gospel tells us that "we are more loved and accepted in Jesus Christ than we ever dared hope."[3]

(9) This is the hope of the gospel.

(10) Even though we are lost in sin, Christ willingly gives his life for us.

(11) He loves us that much.

(12) Christ lived a perfectly righteous life.

(13) Unlike us, he did not deserve God's wrath.

(14) However, he took the wrath that we deserved, and he gave us the love of God that only he deserved.

(15) He imputed his righteousness to us and our guilt to himself.

(16) Since he took our guilt, he also took God's wrath.

(17) Jesus experienced this wrath in his death on the cross.

(18) In this way, Jesus atoned for our sin.

---

2. Timothy Keller with Kath Keller, *The Meaning of Marriage: Facing the Complexities of Commitment with the Wisdom of God* (New York: Dutton, 2011), 44.

3. Keller and Keller, *The Meaning of Marriage*, 44.

(19) We know that the atonement was successful because of the resurrection.

(20) God resurrected Jesus because he accepted Jesus's sacrifice for our sin.

(21) The gospel therefore is about both wrath and love.

(22) Christ loved us so much that he took the wrath that we deserved.

(23) As biblical scholar D. A. Carson writes, "Do you wish to see God's love? Look at the cross. Do you wish to see God's wrath? Look at the cross."[4]

Paragraph 1	*(1) – (3)*
Paragraph 2	
Paragraph 3	
Paragraph 4	

Write a short one-sentence summary of each paragraph.

Paragraph 1	*The gospel is the good news that God has reconciled us to himself through the life, death, and resurrection of Jesus Christ.*
Paragraph 2	
Paragraph 3	
Paragraph 4	

4. D. A. Carson, *The Difficult Doctrine of the Love of God* (Wheaton, IL: Crossway, 2000), 70–71.

4.3 Union with Christ: The Basis of Our Salvation

We are saved by faith. Jesus Christ is the object of our faith, and true faith unites us to Christ by the Holy Spirit. By faith, we have union with Christ. This union is the bond by which we are one with Christ, and he is one with us. Through this union, we do not share in God's divine nature, but we do share in Christ's Sonship. We share in the love that the Father has for the Son. We share in the life of the Trinity. All of the benefits of our salvation, such as justification and sanctification, come from this personal union because all of these benefits come from Christ. Christ Jesus himself is our salvation.

Briefly explain the role that each of the following has in our union with Christ:

Faith	*It is by faith that we are united to Christ.*
The Holy Spirit	
Sonship	
The Father	
Justification and Sanctification	
Christ the Son	

4.4 Grammar Focus: Discourse Connectors

Discourse connectors help organize information. They help readers understand how a sentence relates to the other sentences around it. They help us understand how each sentence comes together to make an argument. Often, they are the first word in a sentence, and sometimes they are separated by commas. The chart below explains some common categories of discourse connectors.[5]

Type of Discourse Connector	What It Indicates	Examples
Ordering	The order or sequence of the points an author makes	first, next, then
Summary	A summary or concluding statement	overall, in summary, in conclusion
Addition	More information to add to a previous point	also, in addition, furthermore, moreover
Exemplification and restatement	Examples or the rewording of a previous point	for example, for instance, that is
Result	What logically follows from a previous argument	accordingly, consequently, therefore
Concession	Information the reader may not expect because of previous information	nevertheless, nonetheless, regardless
Contrast	Information that contradicts or goes against previous information	however, instead, in contrast

Activity

Scan the article below, "Sin and Salvation," and underline each discourse connector. Write down each discourse connector you find next to the correct category below. Note that some of the discourse connecters in the article do not appear in the above chart. An example has been provided.

Ordering	
Summary	

---

5. The following categories and most of the following examples have been taken from Ron Cowan, *The Teacher's Grammar of English: A Course Book and Reference Guide* (Cambridge: Cambridge University Press, 2008), 621–622.

Addition	
Exemplification and restatement	
Result	*therefore,*
Concession	
Contrast	

4.5 Sin and Salvation

Pre-Reading Activity

How would you describe sin?

_____

_____

_____

As you read this article, indicate whether each paragraph speaks mainly of justification, sanctification, or both.

(1) Salvation is God's solution to the problem of sin. Therefore, to understand the fullness of salvation, we must understand the fullness of sin. Sin has two main aspects: (a) guilt and (b) corruption. Accordingly, our union with Christ and the benefits he gives to us must address both the guilt and the corruption that sin causes. Specifically, the benefit of justification addresses sin's guilt and the benefit of sanctification addresses sin's corruption. Let us look at each in turn.

(2) First, guilt is a legal term. Since we have not obeyed God's law, we are guilty before him. However, through our union with Christ, we share in Christ's righteousness. Thus, God declares us righteous, an act that permanently changes our legal status. This act by which a sinner is declared righteous is justification. Yet this is not our own righteousness. It is an alien righteousness. It comes from outside of us. It comes from Christ alone. Nevertheless, we are truly righteous because we are united to Christ, the righteous one.

(3) Second, corruption concerns the ways in which sin has polluted our nature. Sin infects every part of our humanity. That is, no part of us is free from sin's corruption. Even more, because our nature is corrupted by sin, all our actions are sinful. Our sinful nature makes us sin. We are sinners and so we sin. Nonetheless, we choose to sin because we desire to sin. Thus, even our desires are corrupted by sin. However, through our union with Christ, we are sanctified. Unlike justification, sanctification is a process. Sanctification is the process by which the Spirit takes away the corruption of sin and makes us like Christ. This process, though, will not be complete in this life. We must wait for the life to come to be fully free of sin.

(4) Accordingly, we must remember that justification and sanctification work together to address the twofold problem of sin. We are justified by faith alone. We cannot forget that. But since saving faith unites us to Christ, true faith in Christ will produce good works. The same Christ that justifies us is also the Christ that sanctifies us. Therefore, if we are united to him, he will bring about our sanctification, a process that will produce good works. Good works then are the effect and not the cause of salvation.

(5) Furthermore, we see this connection between justification and sanctification in Scripture. For instance, consider chapter 2 of James's letter. At first, James seems to be attacking Paul's doctrine of justification. However, Scripture does not use terms the same way that a theology textbook does. We must pay attention to a writer's specific use of words. When Paul speaks of "works," he speaks of our efforts to save ourselves by our own actions. In contrast, when James speaks of "works," he speaks of the fruit of our salvation. When Paul speaks of "justification," he speaks of God's legal declaration of righteousness. Conversely, when James speaks of "justification," he speaks of the demonstration of the truth of our faith.[6] In fact, Jesus uses the term "justify" in the same way, saying that wisdom will be justified (proved true) by her actions (Matt 11:19; Luke 7:35). In conclusion, James is saying that the good works caused by sanctification will demonstrate the truth of our faith. They will prove that our faith has united us to Christ.

After reading the passage above, complete Chart 1 below.

---

6. For a more detailed explanation of this approach, see Douglas J. Moo, *The Letter of James*, The Pillar New Testament Commentary (Grand Rapids, MI: Eerdmans, 2000), 135. However, it should be noted that Moo ultimately chooses another interpretation of this passage, one that also finds agreement between James and Paul.

Chart 1

Paragraph	Focus: Justification, Sanctification, or Both?	One Important Point from the Paragraph
1		
2		
3		
4		
5		

Complete Chart 2 below. Compare and contrast justification and sanctification using as many terms from the word bank as you can.

Word Bank

union with Christ	corruption	guilt	process	declaration
sin	salvation	benefits	faith	Scripture

Chart 2

List the similarities between justification and sanctification	List the differences between justification and sanctification

Two Soteriological Dangers[7]

When we focus on sanctification without justification, we have the problem of *legalism*. We try to be righteous by our own efforts and improvement. However, God's standard of righteousness is perfection, something we can never achieve. Legalism can never bring us the restful peace of the gospel because it makes us rely on our own work instead of the work of Christ. If we try to be our own savior, then we will never have the confidence and assurance of salvation.

When we focus on justification without sanctification, we encounter the problem of *antinomianism*. We assume that because Christ has given us his righteousness, we do not need to live in a righteous way. We assume that since we are no longer guilty before God, we do not need to obey God. The German theologian and martyr Dietrich Bonhoeffer called this "cheap grace."[8] That is, it does not appreciate what God has done for us. It treats God's grace as if it were cheap, as if it were of no value.

Summarize legalism in one sentence.

_____

_____

_____

Summarize antinomianism in one sentence.

_____

_____

_____

Which of these two dangers do you see most often? Why do you think that is?

_____

_____

_____

_____

---

7. Portions of the following paragraphs have been taken from Cheri Pierson, Will Bankston, and Marilyn Lewis, *Exploring Parables in Luke: Integrated Skills for ESL/EFL Students of Theology* (Carlisle: Langham Global Library, 2014), 11–12.

8. Dietrich Bonhoeffer, *The Cost of Discipleship*, trans. R. H. Fuller and Irmgard Booth (New York: Touchstone, 1995), 43.

4.6 Knowing the Real God and His Salvation

It is sometimes hard for people to love and trust God because they do not know who he really is. Instead of knowing the triune God of Scripture, people often have wrong beliefs about who God is.

Read the following sentences and decide if they are true (T) or false (F).

    (1) God saves us because we are good enough. _F_

    (2) Jesus Christ is only an example of how to live rightly. _____

    (3) Good works come before salvation. _____

    (4) If we are united to Christ, then God loves us as he loves Christ. _____

    (5) If we are saved, then it does not matter how we live. _____

    (6) Certain people are so good that they do not need Christ's righteousness. _____

    (7) What saves us is God's own righteousness, the righteousness of Christ. _____

    (8) We can never be sure that we are good enough and so we can never be sure that we are saved. _____

Choose one false sentence above and explain why this belief is dangerous.

_____

_____

_____

Reading

Below is an excerpt from Michael Reeves's *Delighting in the Trinity*. It is about Martin Luther's discovery of God's grace and love. Do not worry if you do not understand every word. Instead focus on how Luther felt before and after his discovery.

Luther's Great Discovery

The Reformer Martin Luther knew well how much the Fatherhood of God changes the shape of salvation and all our thoughts about God. As a monk, his mind was filled with the knowledge that God is righteous and hates sin, but he failed to see any further into who God is – what his righteousness is and *why* he hates sin.

The result, he said, was that "I did not love, yes, I hated the righteous God who punishes sinners, and secretly . . . I was angry with God."[9] Not knowing God as a kind and willing Father, a God who brings us close, Luther found he could not love him. He and his fellow monks transferred their affections to Mary and various other saints; it was them they would love and to them they would pray.

That changed when he began to see that God is a fatherly God who shares, who gives to us his righteousness, glory and wisdom. Looking back later in life he reflected that, as a monk, he had not actually been worshiping the right God, for it is "not enough," he then said, to know God as the Creator and Judge. Only when God is known as a loving Father is he known [rightly] . . .

Through sending his Son to bring us back to himself, God has revealed himself to be inexpressibly loving and supremely fatherly. What Luther found was that not only does that give great assurance and joy – it also wins our hearts to him, for "we may look into His fatherly heart and sense how boundlessly He loves us."[10] . . . In the salvation of this God we see a God we can really love.[11]

Comprehension Questions

Answer the following questions based on the reading.

(1) What was the main thing that changed Luther's understanding of God?

_____

_____

(2) What did Luther know about God before his discovery?

_____

_____

---

9. Martin Luther, "Preface to the Complete Edition of Luther's Latin Writings," in *Luther's Works*, ed. J. Pelikan (vols. 1–30, St. Louis: Concordia; vols. 31–55, Philadelphia: Fortress, 1955–1976), 34:336–337.

10. Martin Luther, *Luther's Large Catechism* (St. Louis: Concordia, 1978), 70.

11. Michael Reeves, *Delighting in the Trinity: An Introduction to the Christian Faith* (Downers Grove, IL: IVP Academic, 2012), 78–79 (emphasis his).

(3) How did Luther feel about God before his discovery?

_____

_____

(4) Why did Luther pray to Mary and other saints instead of to God?

_____

_____

(5) Where does the righteousness that God gives us come from?

_____

_____

(6) Luther said it was not enough to know God only as creator and judge. How does this relate to the previous chapter's discussion of general revelation?

_____

_____

(7) How did God most fully reveal himself?

_____

_____

(8) Why can we *really* love God?

_____

_____

The Importance of Scripture

Luther made his discovery while reading and lecturing on the Bible. In particular, the books of Galatians and Romans helped him understand the doctrine of justification. This doctrine says that it is by faith alone that we receive the righteousness of God.

Choose one of the following Bible passages: Galatians 2:16; Romans 3:21–31; or Romans 8:1–4. An English translation of each passage is provided below, but you may use a translation in your own language. Fill in the chart below with information from the passage that you chose.

Galatians 2:16

. . . yet we know that a person is not justified by works of the law but through faith in Jesus Christ, so we also have believed in Christ Jesus, in order to be justified by faith in Christ and not by works of the law, because by works of the law no one will be justified.

Romans 3:21–31

But now the righteousness of God has been manifested apart from the law, although the Law and the Prophets bear witness to it – the righteousness of God through faith in Jesus Christ for all who believe. For there is no distinction: for all have sinned and fall short of the glory of God, and are justified by his grace as a gift, through the redemption that is in Christ Jesus, whom God put forward as a propitiation by his blood, to be received by faith. This was to show God's righteousness, because in his divine forbearance he had passed over former sins. It was to show his righteousness at the present time, so that he might be just and the justifier of the one who has faith in Jesus.

Then what becomes of our boasting? It is excluded. By what kind of law? By a law of works? No, but by the law of faith. For we hold that one is justified by faith apart from works of the law. Or is God the God of Jews only? Is he not the God of Gentiles also? Yes, of Gentiles also, since God is one – who will justify the circumcised by faith and the uncircumcised through faith. Do we then overthrow the law by this faith? By no means! On the contrary, we uphold the law.

Romans 8:1–4

There is therefore now no condemnation for those who are in Christ Jesus. For the law of the Spirit of life has set you free in Christ Jesus from the law of sin and death. For God has done what the law, weakened by the flesh, could not do. By sending his own Son in the likeness of sinful flesh and for sin, he condemned sin in the flesh, in order that the righteous requirement of the law might be fulfilled in us, who walk not according to the flesh but according to the Spirit.

Chart

Which passage did you choose?	
What are three important points from this passage?	

Imagine that someone in your church asks you, "How do I know if I have been good enough to be saved?" Use the passage you chose and the chart above to answer this question in the space below.

_____

_____

_____

_____

_____

_____

_____

_____

_____

4.7 Vocabulary

Choose a vocabulary term from this chapter and fill in the boxes below.

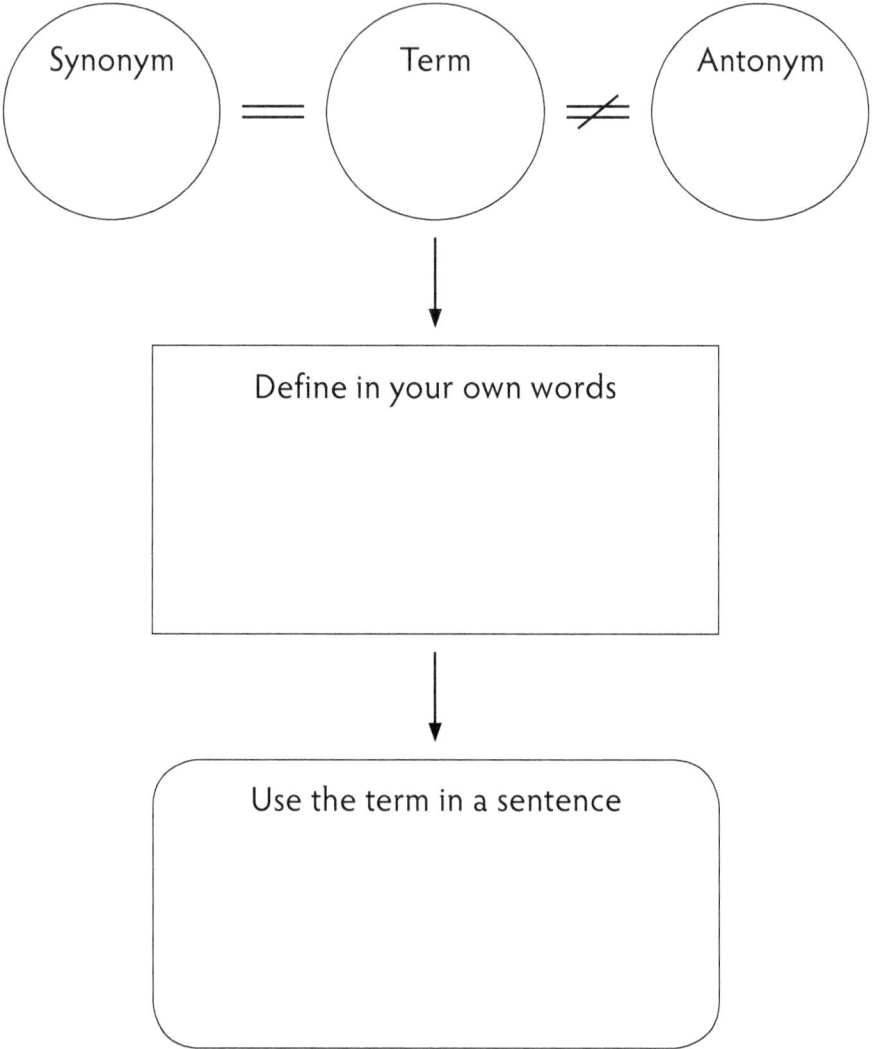

Synonym = Term ≠ Antonym

Define in your own words

Use the term in a sentence

5

Creation

The doctrine of creation tells us what it means to exist as creatures, as beings created by the triune God. God brought all of the universe into existence from nothing, and, as we will see, he did this in order to share his own fullness of life with us. He created all things good, but, through human disobedience, we brought the evil of sin into the world. However, through Christ, God is bringing all of creation back into a right relationship with himself. Join us as we explore how the doctrine of creation relates to theology, Scripture, and the history of the church.

Terms in This Chapter

Aseity (n.)
- The attribute of God that describes his lack of dependence upon anything else and affirms that he has life wholly in and from himself

The created order (noun phrase)
- Another way to speak of God's creation

Creation ex nihilo *(noun phrase)*
- God's act of creation by which he made all things from nothing, from no other pre-existing matter or material (*ex nihilo* is Latin for "from nothing")

The fall (noun phrase)
- The event in which Adam and Eve disobeyed God in the garden of Eden and allowed sin to enter the world

Immanence (n.) / Immanent (adj.)
- The attribute of God that describes his closeness and intimacy to creation as its creator

Transcendence (n.) / Transcendent (adj.)
- The attribute of God that describes his wholly otherness, his complete dissimilarity, from creation as its creator

5.1 Introduction: The Triune Creator

It is important to remember that every Christian doctrine is rooted in the Trinity. Accordingly, we need to understand creation in light of the Trinity. The Bible enables us to understand the act of creation as the act of the triune God.

To begin with, read Genesis 1. Find all of the verses that have the phrase "God said" and write them in the chart below.

	Verse Numbers
"God said . . ."	

Now read John 1:1–5. Jesus here is called the Word. Make notes on what this passage says about the Word in the chart below.

What does John 1:1–5 tells us about the Word?	

Persons perform actions through words. Similarly, God performed his great act of creation through the Word. He spoke, and the Word brought all of creation into existence. Therefore, it was through the Son that God made all things. However, as John 1:1 tells us, the Word is not other than God, but rather he is God himself.

Recall the doctrine of inseparable operations which was discussed in chapter 1. This doctrine tells us that the three persons of the Trinity work together to perform the same action. As theologian Michael Horton writes, "Everything that God does is done by the Father, in the Son, through the Spirit."[1] But, again, these are not different actions. As Horton goes on to explain,

---

1. Michael Horton, *Rediscovering the Holy Spirit: God's Perfecting Presence in Creation, Redemption, and Everyday Life* (Grand Rapids, MI: Zondervan, 2017), 35.

"It is not different *works* but different *roles* in *every work* that the divine persons perform."[2] Therefore, the biblical account of creation paints a picture of the Father creating by speaking the Word.

However, one may ask, what is the Spirit's role in creation? Notice that Genesis 1:2 states that "the Spirit of God was hovering over the face of the waters." Just as the Word is present in the act of creation, so too is the Spirit. It is the role of the Spirit to make divine acts effective and to bring them to perfection. The Spirit brings about the effect of the Word that the Father speaks. As Horton explains, the Spirit's role in the act of creation is to "bring about the intended effect of the Father's command, in the Son,"[3] a role that is just as important as that of the Father and the Son. In particular, "the Spirit gives the kiss of life to mortals in creation," as he makes alive the creation of God.[4] For it is through the Spirit that we receive "the breath of life" and, like Adam, we become "a living creature" (Gen 2:7).

Based on the above reading, decide if the following sentences are true (T) or false (F).

    (1) We need to understand the Trinity to understand the divine act of creation. _T_

    (2) Each person of the Trinity performs different, but related, actions. _____

    (3) The doctrine of inseparable operations is true for all of God's actions. _____

    (4) John 1 helps us to better understand God's act of creation in Genesis 1. _____

    (5) The Spirit's role in creation is more important than the roles of the Father and the Son. _____

    (6) The Father brings about the effect of the Word that the Spirit speaks. _____

    (7) The persons of the Trinity perform different roles, but not different actions. _____

---

2. Horton, *Rediscovering the Holy Spirit*, 38 (emphasis his).

3. Horton, 51.

4. Horton, 56.

Use the chart below to describe the roles that each person of the Trinity plays in divine action.

The Father's Role	
The Son's Role	
The Spirit's Role	

Read the following excerpt from the great hymn about Christ in Colossians 1:

> For by him all things were created, in heaven and on earth, visible and invisible, whether thrones or dominions or rulers or authorities – all things were created through him and for him. And he is before all things, and in him all things hold together. (Col 1:16–17)

Explain how this passage complements Genesis 1 and John 1:1–5 by describing the role of the Son in the divine act of creation.

_____

_____

_____

_____

_____

_____

5.2 The Creator and His Creatures

Grammar Focus 1: Infinitives and Gerunds

An infinitive is formed by *to* + *verb* and a gerund is formed by *verb* + *-ing*. Both infinitives and gerunds (with the phrases that they form) can function as the subject or the object of a sentence:

- To read Scripture is an important activity for Christians.
  - *Note: Generally, only formal, academic writing (such as theological texts) will use an infinitive as the subject of a sentence.*
- Reading Scripture is an important activity for Christians.
- He loves to read the Bible.
- She loves reading the Bible.

An infinitive can also function adverbially to show the purpose of a verb:

- We read Scripture to know God.
- We read Scripture in order to learn about Jesus.

A gerund should not be confused with a present participle. The following sentences contain present participles:

- I am reading the Bible.
- Hearing Jesus, the blind man cried out to him.

The following passage contains several infinitives, gerunds, and present participles. This passage is about God's relation to his creation. Skim the first three paragraphs of the passage and do the following:

- *Underline each infinitive that is the subject or object of a sentence.*
- *Mark each infinitive that indicates purpose in curly brackets.*
- *Circle each gerund.*
- *Mark each present participle within a box.*

(1) One of the most important distinctions in theology is the one that distinguishes the creator from his creation. This is called the creator–creature distinction. God alone is the creator, and all that he has made is his creation. Being created by God, humans are creatures. God exists completely from himself, not needing anything else for his existence. We call this God's aseity. He has complete life in himself. In contrast, humans, like all creatures, rely on God to exist. To be a creature is to be completely dependent upon God for your existence. To be a creature is to exist in a relation of complete dependence upon God. Existing in a state of complete dependence upon God is what makes each

one of us a creature. Being a creature means relying on God for everything. To be a creature, then, is to receive the gift of existence from God himself.

(2) Therefore, the doctrine of creation begins with the doctrine of God. To understand creation, we must understand the creator. Explaining this doctrinal connection, the theologian John Webster writes, "Christian teaching about creation is ordered by confession and acclamation of God's matchless self-sufficiency. In his inner works as Father, Son and Spirit, God is plenitude of life and incomparable excellence."[5] God is matchless in his self-sufficiency because, unlike everything else that exists, he exists completely from himself. Existing in this way also means that God has a plenitude, a complete fullness, of life in himself. Having full joy in the communion of the Father, Son, and Spirit, the triune God creates not to gain joy but to give it. God creates to share with us the fullness of his joyful triune life. To be a creature, then, is to be made to share in God's own plenitude of joy.

(3) The theologian Thomas Weinandy helps us to see how important the title of creator is to rightly understand our relation to God. Weinandy writes, "Creator specifies both the relationship between Yahweh and his creation and simultaneously his radical distinctiveness from creation."[6] Having created us from nothing, God has an incomparably close relationship to us. He knows us and acts upon us more directly than even we know and act upon ourselves. Having given all creatures their existence, he has an incomparable closeness, a matchless intimacy, to each of them. God's closeness, his intimacy, to creation is his immanence. However, the title of creator also communicates the great distinction between God and creation. To speak creation into existence from nothing means that God is completely different from and wholly other than his creation. Theologians call God's act of creating from nothing his creation *ex nihilo*.[7] Only because God is completely different from his creation can he create in this way. The wholly otherness of God is his transcendence. Accordingly, Weinandy shows how God's transcendence (his otherness from us) and his immanence (his closeness to us) work together, rather than against each other. It is because God is wholly other than us that he can be incomparably close to us. It is because he is the transcendent God that he is also the immanent God. As Weinandy writes:

---

5. John Webster, *God without Measure: Working Papers in Christian Theology*, Volume 1: *God and the Works of God* (London; New York: Bloomsbury T&T Clark, 2016), 119.

6. Thomas G. Weinandy, O.F.M. Cap., *Does God Suffer?* (Notre Dame, IN: University of Notre Dame Press, 2000), 48. Yahweh is the covenant name of God in the Old Testament.

7. *Ex nihilo* means "from nothing" in Latin.

(4) The Old Testament never conceives of God's transcendence in opposition to his immanence, as if what makes God wholly other is different from that which allows him to be a personal God who lovingly acts in time and history . . . For God to be transcendent in the biblical understanding means that he is wholly other than the created order but not apart from the created order. That which makes him divine, and thus wholly other and so transcendent, is that which equally allows him to be active within the created order and so be immanent. There is no opposition between God's transcendent being and his immanent activity.[8]

Extensive Reading

After skimming the article and completing the underlining task, read through the first three paragraphs again without the aid of a dictionary. Now summarize the main point of each paragraph in the following chart.

Paragraph	Main Point
1	
2	
3	

---

8. Weinandy, *Does God Suffer?*, 56. Note that "the created order" is another term for creation.

Intensive Reading

Now read carefully through paragraph 4. This is a direct quote from a challenging theological text. Based on this quotation, define God's transcendence and his immanence in your own words.

Divine transcendence:

_____

_____

_____

Divine immanence:

_____

_____

_____

Grammar Focus 2: Infinitives and Gerunds

When using infinitives and gerunds as the object of a sentence, it is important to remember that certain verbs take infinitives as their object and other verbs take gerunds as their object.

The chart below provides a sampling of verbs that take an infinitive as their object.[9]

agree	fail	learn	refuse
appear	hope	need	wait
ask	intend	plan	want
decide	know how	promise	wish

- He <u>agreed to attend</u> the lecture.
- She <u>appears to disagree</u> with the argument.
- They <u>failed to make</u> their argument.
- I <u>intend to research</u> that doctrine.
- I <u>want to read</u> more about that topic.

---

9. The examples of verbs from the three following charts have been taken from Keith S. Folse, *Keys to Teaching Grammar to English Language Learners: A Practical Handbook*, 2nd ed. (Ann Arbor, MI: University of Michigan Press, 2016), 245–246.

The chart below provides a sampling of verbs that take a gerund as their object.

appreciate	deny	insist on	quit
avoid	discuss	mention	recommend
consider	dislike	miss	suggest
delay	enjoy	practice	think about

- The students <u>avoided making</u> errors.
- The professor <u>delayed giving</u> his lecture.
- The researcher <u>disliked reading</u> books by that author.
- He <u>recommended using</u> flash cards to study Hebrew.
- She <u>suggested researching</u> that doctrine for my essay.

In addition, only gerunds will follow a preposition:

- The professor thanked the students <u>for working</u> hard.
- For the class, studying grammar was the most difficult part <u>of learning</u> Greek.
- The author succeeded <u>at proving</u> his point.
- The essay did a lot <u>of wandering</u> from its main topic.

Note that some verbs can take both infinitives and gerunds as their object. The chart below provides a sampling of such verbs.

begin	hate	love
continue	like	prefer

- I <u>began to study</u> theology three years ago.
- I <u>began studying</u> theology three years ago.
- I <u>will continue to research</u> that doctrine.
- I <u>will continue researching</u> that doctrine.

With the aid of the above section, complete the following paragraph with the infinitive form of the verb, the gerund form of the verb, or both. Also remember that these rules apply only when an infinitive or a gerund is the object of a verb.

The creator–creature distinction intends _____(distinguish)

God from everything he has created. When we fail _____(make)

this distinction, we insist on _____(reject) both who God

is and who we are. _____ (deny) this distinction is a case of _____ (commit) idolatry. We like _____ (think of) ourselves as the ones who have aseity. However, the fact that we are dependent upon God for our very existence is a wonderful truth. As John Webster explains, _____ (embrace) this truth is _____ (realize) that God loves _____ (share) his own fullness of joy. The Father, Son, and Spirit eternally enjoy _____ (commune) with one another, and it is this joy that God intends _____ (lavish) upon us as his creatures. Therefore, we must avoid _____ (think) that God created us to gain a joy that he was missing. Instead, the fullness of God's delight in himself is the basis of _____ (understand) the doctrine of creation. We can only appreciate _____ (exist) as wholly dependent upon him when we learn _____ (recognize) the fullness of joy he intends _____ (give) to us. This is the very purpose for which the Father sent his Son, _____ (save) us from our sin and _____ (bring) us back into a right relationship with himself. _____ (be) united to Christ is _____ (participate) in the triune communion of the Father, Son, and Holy Spirit.

Now add two final sentences to the above paragraph using at least two infinitives and two gerunds.

_____

_____

_____

_____

_____

_____

5.3 The Goodness of Creation and the Problem of Sin

Read again through Genesis 1.

How many times does God describe what he created as good? _____

Everything he created existed in a right relationship to him. Every part of creation fulfilled the purposes that God had for it.

Maximus the Confessor explains why this must be true. He writes, "For if anyone said that something natural had resisted God, this would be rather a charge against God than against nature, for introducing war naturally to the realm of being and raising up insurrection against himself and strife among all that exists."[10]

Take a moment to think about this quote.

How would you define Maximus's use of "natural"?

_____

_____

_____

Paraphrase this quote in your own words.

_____

_____

_____

If creation was *not* created good by God, why would God be at fault for the evil we see in the world?

_____

_____

_____

Since God is not at fault for evil, and since everything he created was good, why is there evil in the world?

_____

_____

_____

10. Maximus the Confessor, *Opuscule 7*, in Andrew Louth, *Maximus the Confessor* (London; New York: Routledge, 1996), 185.

This is a difficult question, and only the Bible can give us the correct answer. As Albert Wolters writes, "The great danger is always to single out some aspect or phenomenon of God's good creation and identify it, rather than the alien intrusion of human apostasy, as the villain in the drama of human life."[11] What Wolters is saying is that, apart from the Bible, we will always point to some good thing that God created as the reason why there is evil in the world. For instance, many thinkers throughout history have blamed the body for the evils in the world. However, God created the human body and called it good. We might misuse the body, but that does not make the body an evil thing. To say that the body is evil is to make the mistake that Maximus warns us against. To make this error is to say that God is at fault for the evil in the world. Therefore, the answer to the above question must be something that is not a part of creation. The only answer we can give is sin, which is not a part of creation, but, instead, something that has infected creation. When Adam and Eve listened to Satan and disobeyed God in the garden of Eden, they enabled sin to enter God's good creation. Since then, creation has not existed in a right relationship to God, and humans have put creation to purposes that stand against God's own purposes. As slaves to sin, we have become sinners. For instance, we willingly misuse the good gift of the body that God has given us.

What are other parts of creation that people have blamed for the evil in the world?

_____

_____

_____

_____

The theologian Karl Barth makes a similar point to Wolters. Barth writes of sin, "Of itself, the creature cannot recognize this encounter and what it encounters. It experiences and endures it. But it also misinterprets it, as has always happened."[12] What Barth is saying is that while we constantly experience the effects of sin, we do not know what we are experiencing. We always identify the evil effects of sin on us and the world as a result of something else. Only Scripture can enable us to rightly identify this "something" as sin. In particular,

---

11. Albert M. Wolters, *Creation Regained: Biblical Basics for a Reformational Worldview*, 2nd ed. (Grand Rapids, MI: Eerdmans, 2005), 61.

12. Karl Barth, *Church Dogmatics*, Volume III/3: *The Doctrine of Creation*, trans. and ed. G. W. Bromiley and G. T. Thomson (London; New York: Bloomsbury T&T Clark, 1960), 350.

as Barth writes of sin, "The creature knows it only as it knows God in His being and attitude against it."[13] That is to say, we know sin by implication of God's action against it. We know how evil it is because Scripture tells us how much God hates it. We know of the deep corruption and guilt that sin has imparted to us because we know that only Christ's death and resurrection could rescue us from it. We know that we will not always be victims of sin because we know that God is purifying us from sin through sanctification. We know that God will destroy sin because we know that there will be no sin when Christ returns and fully restores God's good creation.

Based on the above reading, complete the following chart.

Summarize in one sentence the above reading's explanation of sin and its effects upon the world	
Give three supporting details for your summary	

Supporting Detail 1:	Supporting Detail 2:	Supporting Detail 3:

---

13. Barth, *Church Dogmatics* III/3, 350.

5.4 Creation and the Goodness of Work

Pre-Reading Activity

What are common jobs and careers in your context?

_____

_____

_____

_____

Think about one of these jobs or careers. What benefits does this job bring to the world?

_____

_____

_____

_____

In the following excerpt from his book *Every Good Endeavor*, Timothy Keller points out that a correct doctrine of creation shows us the goodness and importance of work.

Read this passage and then answer the questions that follow.

> *Excerpt 1*
>
> The book of Genesis leaves us with a striking truth – work was part of paradise. One biblical scholar summed it up: "It is perfectly clear that God's good plan always included human beings working, or, more specifically, living in the constant cycle of work and rest."[14] . . . Work did not come in after a golden age of leisure. It was part of God's perfect design for human life, because we were made in God's image, and part of his glory and happiness is that he works, as does the Son of God, who said, "My Father is always at his work to this very day, and I too am working" (John 5:17).
>
> The fact that God put work in paradise is startling to us because we so often think of work as a necessary evil or even

_____

14. Ben Witherington, *Work: A Kingdom Perspective on Labor* (Grand Rapids, MI: Eerdmans, 2011), 2.

punishment. Yet we do not see work brought into our human story after the fall of Adam, as part of the resulting brokenness and curse; it is part of the blessedness of the garden of God. Work is as much a basic human need as food, beauty, rest, friendship, prayer, and sexuality; it is not simply medicine but food for our soul. Without meaningful work we sense significant inner loss and emptiness.[15]

Questions

Keller's argument for the goodness of work is based on the fact that work came before *the fall*. That is, it came before Adam and Eve sinned in the garden. Why must work be good if it existed prior to the fall?

_____

_____

_____

What role does the fact that we are created in God's image play in Keller's argument? How does he use this truth to make a connection between our activity and God's activity?

_____

_____

_____

Is Keller's position a common understanding of work? Why or why not?

_____

_____

_____

How might you explain this understanding of work to people in your church?

_____

_____

_____

---

15. Timothy Keller with Katherine Leary Alsdorf, *Every Good Endeavor: Connecting Your Work to God's Work* (New York: Dutton, 2012), 36–37.

Now read a second excerpt from the same book and answer the questions that follow.

Excerpt 2

Nevertheless, it is meaningful that God himself rested after work (Genesis 2:2). Many people make the mistake of thinking that work is a curse and that something else (leisure, family, or even "spiritual" pursuits) is the only way to find meaning in life. The Bible, as we have seen and will see, exposes the lie of this idea. But it also keeps us from falling into the opposite mistake, namely, that work is the only important human activity and that rest is a necessary evil – something we do strictly to "recharge our batteries" in order to continue to work. We look to what we know about God to make this case. He did not need any restoration of his strength – and yet he rested on the seventh day (Genesis 2:1–3). As beings made in his image, then, we can assume that rest, and the things you do as you rest, are good and life-giving in and of themselves. Work is not all there is to life. You will not have a meaningful life without work, but you cannot say that your work is *the* meaning of your life. If you make any work the purpose of your life – even if that work is church ministry – you create an idol that rivals God. Your relationship with God is the most important foundation for your life, and indeed it keeps all the other factors – work, friendships and family, leisure and pleasure – from becoming so important to you that they become addicting and distorted.[16]

Questions

Based on the context, what does Keller mean by the following phrases?

- a necessary evil

  _____

  _____

- recharge our batteries

  _____

  _____

---

16. Keller, *Every Good Endeavor*, 40 (emphasis his).

- life-giving

  _____

  _____

- idol

  _____

  _____

If the first excerpt argued for the importance of work, what is the main idea of the second excerpt?

_____

_____

_____

How do both excerpts work together to give us a correct understanding of work?

_____

_____

_____

Which error is more common in your context: seeing work as unimportant or making work an idol? Why do you think that is?

_____

_____

_____

How would you summarize the two excerpts for someone who makes the more common error in your context?

_____

_____

_____

5.5 Vocabulary

Choose a vocabulary term from this chapter and fill in the boxes below.

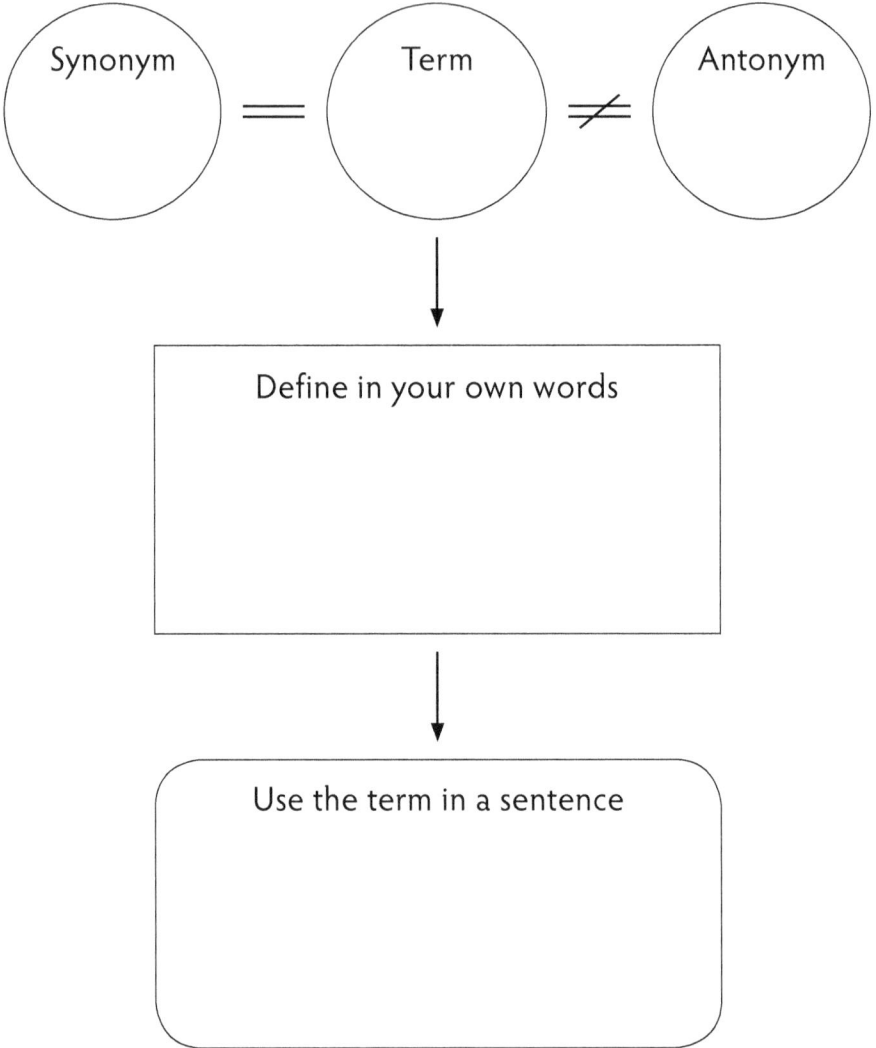

Synonym = Term ≠ Antonym

Define in your own words

Use the term in a sentence

Conclusion

> If you put these things before the brothers, you will be a good servant of Christ Jesus, being trained in the words of the faith and of the good doctrine that you have followed.
> 1 Timothy 4:6

Congratulations! Because of your diligence, you have completed this curriculum of five foundational doctrines of the Christian faith: the Trinity, Christology, revelation and Scripture, soteriology, and creation. Each doctrine is essential for believers to understand, and we must relate each doctrine to our broader theology, Scripture, and the history of the church. What follows is a brief review of the five doctrines.

In chapter 1 we explored the doctrine of the Trinity that tells us who God is. To understand Christian theology, we begin by understanding the triune God. The Trinity is the foundation of all that we believe as Christians.

In chapter 2 we explored the doctrine of Jesus Christ (Christology) which focuses on who Jesus is and what he has done. This doctrine relates directly to the Trinity because God the Son became human to save us.

In chapter 3 we explored the doctrine of revelation and Scripture which tells us how God communicates himself to us. He communicates himself as creator through the general revelation of creation. However, through the special revelation of Scripture he communicates himself as both creator and redeemer.

In chapter 4 we explored the doctrine of salvation (soteriology) which tells us what God has done in Jesus Christ to reconcile sinners to himself. The Holy Spirit unites us to Christ by faith, enabling us to share in the love and life of the Trinity.

In chapter 5 we explored the doctrine of creation which tells us what it means to exist as beings created by the triune God. God brought all that exists into being from nothing, and he created all things good. However, through disobedience, humankind brought the evil of sin into the world. Through Christ, God is bringing all of creation back into a right relationship with himself.

Concluding Tasks

We hope that in this conclusion you will be able to put into practice that which you have been learning throughout this curriculum. By reading, writing, listening, and speaking, you will be able to understand and communicate these doctrines more clearly. Reflect on the following questions. Write down some insights and then share your responses with a partner.

Read the following verses. Then write a response to the question below.

1 Timothy 4:6 If you put these things before the brothers, you will be a good servant of Christ Jesus, being trained in the words of the faith and of the good doctrine that you have followed.
2 Timothy 3:16–17 All Scripture is breathed out by God and profitable for teaching, for reproof, for correction, and for training in righteousness, that the man of God may be complete, equipped for every good work.
2 Timothy 4:3 For the time is coming when people will not endure sound teaching, but having itching ears they will accumulate for themselves teachers to suit their own passions . . .
Titus 2:1 But as for you, teach what accords with sound doctrine.
Titus 2:7 Show yourself in all respects to be a model of good works, and in your teaching show integrity, dignity . . .
Question: Based on the verses above, why is it important for Christians to explore and understand doctrine?

(1) How has this curriculum deepened your understanding of these five basic doctrines of the Christian faith?

_____

_____

_____

_____

(2) Choose one of the five doctrines above. Summarize three key points of this doctrine and write them in the diagram below.

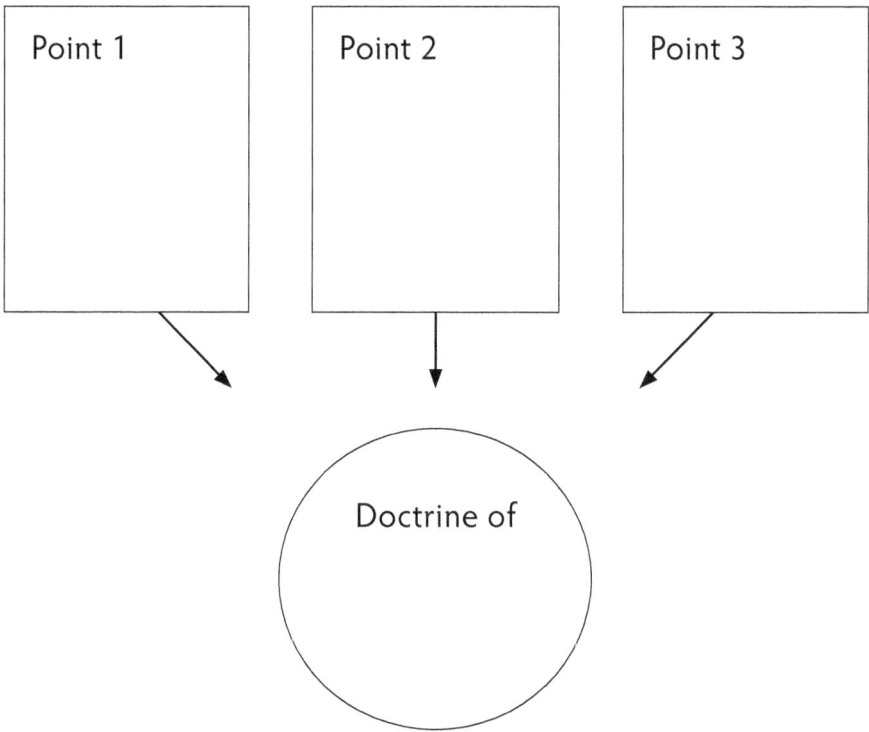

Point 1	Point 2	Point 3

Doctrine of

(3) Discuss your three points with a partner. Ask him or her to critique your points. Write your partner's suggestions below.

_____

_____

_____

(4) Prepare an outline on a separate sheet of paper. Points 1, 2, and 3 will be your major headings.

I.   **Introduction**

II.   **Point 1**

    a.   Supporting Detail

    b.   Supporting Detail

III. **Point 2**

    a.   Supporting Detail

    b.   Supporting Detail

IV.   **Point 3**

    a.   Supporting Detail

    b.   Supporting Detail

V.   **Conclusion**

(5) Prepare a short presentation. Use your outline to complete the chart below. Prepare the presentation. Then present it to your class or small group.

Presenter	
Doctrine	
Introduction	
1st Point (summarize the 1st point)	
2nd Point (summarize the 2nd point)	
3rd Point (summarize the 3rd point)	
Important Vocabulary (Include key terms associated with this doctrine)	
Conclusion & Questions (Think about possible questions you may need to answer from your peers)	

Answer Key

Questions with subjective answers might not appear here.

Chapter 1: Trinity

1.1 Introduction

- What is an example of a *polytheistic* religion?

  Hinduism is an example of a polytheistic religion.

- Is Christianity *monotheistic* or *polytheistic*?

  Christianity is monotheistic.

- As Christians, we worship one *God* in three *persons*.
- What does *eternal* mean?

  To be eternal is to be without beginning or end.

1.3 Trinitarian Heresies

Exercise

(1) In contrast to the Father, there was a time when the Son did not exist. *Arianism*

(2) God's one-ness and his three-ness are equally important. *Orthodox*

(3) Now God appears to us as the Holy Spirit. *Modalism*

(4) Jesus lived such a good life that he became God's Son. *Adoptionism*

(5) The Father, the Son, and the Spirit all have the same divine nature. *Orthodox*

(6) The Son was created and is not eternal with the Father. *Arianism*

(7) Jesus is greater than us, but he is still part of creation. *Arianism*

(8) Jesus is like God. *Arianism*

(9) God is really one person and only seems to be three distinct persons. *Modalism*

(10)   There was never a time when the Son and the Spirit did not exist with the Father. *Orthodox*

(11)   God once showed himself as the Father and then as the Son and now as the Spirit. *Modalism*

(12)   God did not become a human. A human became God. *Adoptionism*

1.4 Grammar Focus: Relative Clauses and Counterfactual Conditionals

Grammar Focus 1: Relative Clauses

Exercise: Underlining Relative Clauses

Excerpt 1 from Michael Reeves's Delighting in the Trinity

"Father," says Jesus the Son in John 17:24, "you loved *me* before the creation of the world." The eternal Son, <u>who according to Colossians 1 is "before all things"</u> (Col 1:17), the one through whom <u>"all things were created"</u> (Col 1:16), the one Hebrews 1 calls "Lord" and "God," <u>who "laid the foundations of the earth"</u> (Heb 1:10) – it is he <u>who is loved by the Father before the creation of the world.</u> The Father, then, is the Father of the eternal Son, and he finds his very identity, his Fatherhood, in loving and giving out his life and being to the Son.

Write three relative clauses that could complete the following sentence (answers may vary):
The Son (1), *who is begotten by the Father,* is Jesus Christ.
(2), *who lived as a man in Nazareth,* is Jesus Christ.
(3), *who was with the Father before all things,* is Jesus Christ.

Grammar Focus 2: Counterfactual Conditionals

Exercise: Circling the Conditional Clause and Underlining the Result Clause of Each Counterfactual Conditional

Excerpt 2 from Michael Reeves's Delighting in the Trinity

(Conditional clauses have been highlighted and result clauses have been underlined.)

Now, <u>God could not *be* love</u> if there were nobody to love. He could not be a Father without a child. And yet it is not as if God created so *that* he could love someone. He *is* love, and does not need to create in order to be who he is . . . If he created us in order to be who he is, _we_ would be giving _him_ life.

That is why it is important to note that the Son is the _eternal Son_. There was never a time when he didn't exist. If there were, then God is a completely different sort of being.

If there were once a time when the Son didn't exist, then there was once a time when the Father was not yet a Father. And if that is the case, then once upon a time God was not loving since all by himself he would have had nobody to love.

Exercise (Answers may vary)

(1) If God were only one person, then the Son would not be the eternal Son.

(2) If God had created us so that he could love someone, he would not be love himself.

(3) If there were a time when the Son did not exist, then the Father would not be the eternal Father.

Review the above section on Trinitarian heresies to complete the following result clauses (answers may vary):

(1) If Adoptionism were true, then the Son would have become the Son during Jesus's earthly life.

(2) If Modalism were true, then the Son would be one of the three ways in which God appears to us.

(3) If Arianism were true, then the Son would have been created by the Father.

1.5 Biblical Exegesis of the Trinity

Warm-Up

[5]Have this mind among yourselves, which is yours in Christ Jesus, who though he was in the form of God, did not count equality with God a thing to be grasped, but emptied himself, by taking the form of a servant, being born in the likeness of men. And being found in human form, he humbled himself by becoming obedient to the point of death, even death on a cross.

1.6 The Council of Nicaea and Pro-Nicene Theology (Answers in this section may vary)

Exercise

Paragraph 1: The Council of Nicaea was called because of the teachings of Arianism, and the council decided that the Son and the Father had the same nature.

Paragraph 2: Pro-Nicene theologians believe that if you say something about God's nature, it applies to all three persons, and that the Son and the Father are not two gods.

Paragraph 3: The third important belief that pro-Nicene theologians hold is that the three persons of the Trinity work together as one.

Paragraph 4: Inseparable operations demonstrated to Gregory that God is three persons in one nature, and that the three persons always act in unity.

Paragraph 5: These theologians believed that the best way to know about God is to look at his actions.

Whole passage: The Council of Nicaea met to discuss and prove wrong a heretical teaching about the Trinity, and decided that God is three persons in one nature, and that his nature is revealed through his actions.

Chapter 2: Christology

2.2 Classic Formulations

(1) The Trinity exists as _three_ persons in _one_ nature.

(2) Christ exists as _one_ person in _two_ natures.

2.3 The Attributes of God

Exercise

(1) Attributes:

   b. characteristics or words of description (in this case of God)

(2) Omniscient:

   a. all-knowing, or knowing everything

(3) Omnipotent:

   c. all-powerful, or the most powerful

(4) Eternal:

a. existing forever

(5) Faithful:

b. trustworthy

Vocabulary Strategies

What do these words have in common? _They all begin with omni-._

Practice

Word	Definition
omnipotent	all-powerful
omniscient	all-knowing
omnipresent	all-present

faith	grace	kind	right	truth
faithful	graceful	kinder	rightful	truly
faithless	graceless	kindness	righteous	truthful

2.4 The Importance of Sending

Fill in the Blanks

In Time (the Economic Trinity)
- The Father sends the Son.
- The Father and Son send the Spirit.

In Eternity (the Immanent Trinity)
- The Father begets the Son.
- The Spirit proceeds from the Father and the Son.

2.5 Grammar Focus: Comparisons

Exercise

(1) God is _wiser_ than humanity.

(2) God is _stronger_ than humanity.

(3) God is *more faithful* than humanity.

(4) God is *more glorious* than humanity.

(5) God's words are *more dependable* than our words.

(6) God's promises are *more trustworthy* than ours.

(7) God's works are *mightier* than our works.

(8) God's words are *more certain* than those of humanity.

(9) God's plans are *better* than our plans.

(10) Christ's blood is *more precious* than any other sacrifice.

(11) Christ's human birth was *humbler* than we expected.

2.6 Augustine's Exegesis

Pre-Reading Activities

(1) Jesus's human nature is <u>less</u> powerful than his divine nature.

(2) Understanding Christ's two natures is <u>more</u> complex than understanding our one nature.

Reading: Underlining Each Occurrence of "Equal to" and "Less Than"

The church father Augustine gives us a hermeneutical rule for understanding Christ's speech in Scripture and passages about him in Scripture. It is a "rule of interpretation." It states that "the Son is <u>equal to</u> the Father in the form of God" and "<u>less than</u> the Father in the form of man." Therefore, when we read an utterance of or about Jesus in Scripture, we must ask if the passage communicates according to the form of God or according to the form of man (the form of a human servant). As Augustine writes, if "we know this rule for understanding the scriptures about God's Son and can . . . distinguish . . . them, one tuned to the form of God in which he . . . is <u>equal to</u> the Father, the other tuned to the form of a servant which he took and is <u>less than</u> the Father, [then] we will not be upset by statements in the holy books that appear to [contradict] each other."

Augustine explains this rule by looking at specific passages. He writes, "In the form of God the Son is <u>equal to</u> the Father, and so is the Holy Spirit, since neither of them is a creature . . . In the form of a servant, however, he is <u>less than</u> the Father, because he himself said 'The Father is greater than I' (John 14:28); he is also <u>less than</u> himself, because it is said of him that 'he emptied himself' (Phil 2:7); and he is <u>less than</u> the Holy Spirit, because he himself said, 'Whoever utters a blasphemy against the Son of man, it will be forgiven him; but whoever utters one against the Holy Spirit, it will not be forgiven him' (Matt 12:32)."

Identifying the Main Ideas

_____ (1) How we read the Bible is important.

___✓___ (2) Christ speaks in two different ways according to his two different natures.

_____ (3) We need the Bible to understand our sin.

_____ (4) Augustine had many struggles in his life.

___✓___ (5) When Jesus's words seem contradictory, we must know that he is both human and divine.

___✓___ (6) We must understand who Christ is to understand what he is saying.

_____ (7) The Holy Spirit is a person in the Trinity.

_____ (8) Reading Scripture every day is important.

Passage	Form of God or Humanity?
"All things were made through him, and without him was not any thing made that was made" (John 1:3)	_God_
"My soul is very sorrowful, even to death" (Matt 26:38)	_Human_
Christ came "not to do [his] own will but the will of him who sent [him]" (John 6:38)	_Human_
"I and the Father are one" (John 10:30)	_God_
Christ was "born of woman, under the law" (Gal 4:4)	_Human_
"For as the Father has life in himself, so he has granted the Son also to have life in himself" (John 5:26)	_God_
"He is the true God and eternal life" (1 John 5:20)	_God_
"He humbled himself by becoming obedient to the point of death, even death on a cross" (Phil 2:8)	_Human_
"All that the Father has is mine" (John 15:16)	_God_

2.7 The Council of Chalcedon: Before and After

Pre-Reading Activity: **Highlighting the First Occurrences of the Council of Chalcedon, the Council of Nicaea, Cyril, and Maximus**

The Council of Chalcedon was convened in AD 451 and it built upon the Council of Nicaea, which took place in AD 325. While Nicaea focused mainly on the doctrine of the Trinity, Chalcedon focused upon Christology. As Lewis Ayres points out, a core belief of pro-Nicaean theologians was that if something belonged to the divine nature, then it was one and it belonged to the three divine persons in the same way. For instance, each of the divine attributes describes the one divine nature. When we say that God is eternal, we are speaking of the divine nature that is shared by the Father, Son, and Holy Spirit. On the other hand, when we speak of "being begotten," we are speaking only of the Son. Accordingly, the distinction between person and nature became very important in understanding both the Trinity and Jesus Christ.

Before Nicaea, a controversy arose between Cyril of Alexandria (c. AD 376–444) and Nestorius regarding how many persons are in Christ. Nestorius claimed that there are two persons in Christ, a divine person and a human person. Cyril feared that this formulation meant that there were two Sons, rather than the one Son of God. He argued for the hypostatic union – that Christ's divine and human natures were united in the one divine person, who is the Son of God, the Logos himself. And it is important to note that when Cyril speaks of a human nature, he speaks of a human body, mind, and soul. At the incarnation, when the Son of God became human, he took every part of our humanity.

Cyril's understanding of the term "person" is that of an actor, an agent, a center of action. He writes, "both the manly as well as the godly sayings were uttered by one subject" – that is, both the divine actions and the human actions were the actions of one divine person. As John McGuckin explains of Cyril's Christology, there is "only one personal subject of the divine and human actions." Therefore, Christ's one person acts through his two natures to produce two different kinds of actions. Eventually Cyril's theology was accepted as the orthodox formulation at the Council of Ephesus in AD 431. Then, twenty years later, the Council of Chalcedon further distinguished Christ's one person and two natures. That is, while the Trinity exists as three persons in one nature, Christ exists as two natures in one person.

After Chalcedon, another controversy arose known as the Monothelite Controversy. Monothelite is a Greek term that means "one will." The Monothelites believed that Christ has only one will. However, Maximus the Confessor

(c. AD 580–662) fought against Monothelitism and argued for Dyothelitism, a Greek term meaning "two wills." He believed that Christ has two wills. This is because Maximus understood the will to be part of one's nature and not a part of one's person. Therefore, since Jesus has two natures, he has two wills. But what exactly is a *will* in Maximus's theology? In Maximus's formulation, the will produces desires that agree with one's nature. It makes us desire certain things and we act to fulfill these desires as persons. The nature produces desires through the will and the person chooses to act on these desires.

This might seem like an unimportant formulation, but Maximus uses it to understand many texts about Jesus in the Bible. For example, when John 1:43 speaks of Jesus going into Galilee, this can only be an action from the human will because God is by nature "absent from no place." In "going" he was acting on a desire from his human will. The divine will cannot desire to go to a particular place because the divine nature is omnipresent. The divine nature is already in every place. Similarly, when Jesus says, "I thirst," on the cross (John 19:28), or when he speaks of his wish to eat the Passover meal with his disciples (Luke 22:15), he is communicating the desires of his human nature. Only the human nature in Christ, and not the divine nature, desires food and drink. However, in Matthew 23:37 and Luke 13:34, Jesus communicates his desire to gather the people of Jerusalem as a hen gathers her chicks. Maximus points out that this desire is divine because (1) it describes God's desire to be with his people, and (2) this desire is older than the human nature of Jesus. This supports Chalcedonian orthodoxy and helps us better understand how Christ's one divine person acts through his two natures.

Putting It Together (Answers may vary)

- The Council of Nicaea: Focused on the doctrine of the Trinity
- Cyril of Alexandria: The one person of Christ acts according to both his divine nature and human nature
- The Council of Chalcedon: Focused on the doctrine of Christology
- Maximus the Confessor: Dyothelitism – two wills; desires are based on your will

Chapter 3: Revelation and Scripture

3.1 Two Kinds of Revelation (Answers in this section may vary)

Compare and contrast inspiration and illumination in the chart below.

List differences between inspiration and illumination	List similarities between inspiration and illumination
Inspiration took place in the past, whereas illumination takes place in the present Inspiration helped the authors write the Bible, while illumination helps readers understand the Bible	Both inspiration and illumination come from the Holy Spirit

3.2 Redemptive History

Phase of Redemptive History	Section of the Bible
Creation	Genesis 1–2
Fall	Genesis 3
Redemption	Genesis 3:14 – Revelation
Consummation	Revelation

Describe the promise made by God to Adam and Eve in one sentence:

God promised to curse the serpent and bless humanity.

Describe the fulfillment of this promise in one sentence:

The fulfillment is the victory of Jesus Christ.

3.3 Grammar Focus: Complements with "That"

Scan for complements: Underlining all of the "that" complements.

God's Promise and Fulfillment

After Adam and Eve disobey God, God does two things in one action. God says to the devil, "I will put enmity between you and the woman, and between your offspring and her offspring; he shall bruise your head, and you shall bruise his heal" (Gen 3:15). This promise of "bruising" is a curse of defeat on the serpent and a promise of hope to Adam to Eve. Or, as one writer says, "The deliverance of God's people always comes through the destruction of God's enemies." God's people are saved when God's enemies are defeated. God promises <u>that the devil will be destroyed,</u> and <u>that God's people will be saved</u>. But who is this offspring who will curse the devil and bless God's people? Who is the one who will fulfill this promise? He is the one who will represent all of God's people as their head. However, his heal will be bruised. He will be wounded by Satan.

The Bible says <u>that this promise of cursing the serpent and blessing humanity</u> was fulfilled in Jesus Christ. He is the one who was bruised by the devil. The Old Testament tells us <u>that the promised one will suffer</u>. For instance, consider Isaiah 52–53. However, people did not understand the importance of suffering in the ministry of the Messiah, the Christ. For example, in Matthew 16, after Peter has rightly identified Jesus as the Christ, Peter then rebukes Jesus when Jesus speaks of his coming death. At that time, Peter could not understand <u>that the Christ would be bruised and would suffer</u>.

However, Jesus's suffering is the "means by which God will restore his people." We are saved through the wounding of Christ. When Christ suffered on the cross, he "disarmed the rulers and authorities and put them to open shame, by triumphing over them" (Col 2:15). Like Peter, the demonic powers did not understand how Christ would fulfill God's promise. When Jesus Christ died on the cross, Satan believed <u>that he had defeated Jesus</u>. But the cross was actually the defeat of Satan. The church also is a part of the bruising of the devil. Paul promises the church, "The God of peace will soon crush Satan under your feet" (Rom 16:20).

3.5 Typology and Reading Scripture

Pre-Reading Questions (Answers may vary)

Work with a partner to answer the following questions:

Explain how Christ fulfills another Old Testament role or institution (such as the temple or sacrificial system).

> *Examples: the role of the sacrifice, the role of the king, the role of the prophet, the role of the priest.*

The following article does not use the word *typology*. However, skim the article and identify which paragraph speaks of Christ's typological roles. Write your answer below.

The last paragraph.

Pre-Reading Activity

Scan the following reading and underline each "that" *complement. Underlined below.*

Excerpt from Michael Reeves's Delighting in the Trinity

(1) . . . the point of all the Scriptures is to make Christ known. As the Son makes his Father known, so the Spirit-breathed Scriptures make the Son known. Paul wrote to Timothy of how "from infancy you have known the holy Scriptures, which are able to make you wise for salvation through faith in Christ Jesus" (2 Tim 3:15). He is referring to the Old Testament, of course, but the same could be said of the New. Similarly, Jesus said to the Jews of his day: "You diligently study the Scriptures because you think that by them you possess eternal life. These are the Scriptures that testify about me, yet you refuse to come to me to have life . . . If you believed Moses, you would believe me, for he wrote about me" (Jn 5:39–40, 46). Clearly, Jesus believed that it is quite possible to study the Scriptures diligently and entirely miss their point, which is to proclaim him so that readers might come to him for life.

(2) It all dramatically affects why we open the Bible. We can open our Bibles for all sorts of odd reasons – as a religious duty, an attempt to earn God's favor, or thinking that it serves as a moral self-help guide, a manual of handy tips for effective religious lives. That idea is actually one main reason so many feel discouraged in their Bible-reading. Hoping to find quick lessons for how they should spend today, people find instead a genealogy, or a list of various sacrifices. And how could page after page of histories, descriptions of the temple, instructions to priests, affect how I rest, work and pray today?

(3) But when you see that Christ is the subject of all the Scriptures, that he is the Word, the Lord, the Son who reveals his Father, the promised Hope, the true Temple, the true Sacrifice, the great High Priest, the ultimate King, then you can read, not so much asking, "What does this mean for me, right now?" but

"What do I learn here of Christ?" Knowing <u>that the Bible is about him and not me</u> means <u>that, instead of reading the Bible obsessing about me, I can gaze on him</u>. And as through the pages you get caught up in the wonder of his story, you find your heart strangely pounding for him in a way you never would have if you had treated the Bible as a book about you.

Chapter 4: Soteriology

4.1 Introduction: Good News and Good Advice (Answers in this section may vary)

Is the gospel good news or good advice? Why?

Good news. It's about what Jesus has done.

4.2 The Gospel and the Cross (Answers in this section may vary)

Dividing the sentences into paragraphs.

Paragraph 1	*(1)–(3)*
Paragraph 2	*(4)–(11)*
Paragraph 3	*(12)–(20)*
Paragraph 4	*(21)–(23)*

4.3 Union with Christ: The Basis of Our Salvation

Briefly explain the role that each of the following has in our union with Christ.

Faith	*It is by faith that we are united to Christ.*
The Holy Spirit	*The Holy Spirit unites us to Christ through our faith.*
Sonship	*We share in Christ's Sonship because we receive the love of the Father for the Son.*
The Father	*The Father loves us as he loves the Son.*
Justification and Sanctification	*Benefits of salvation that come from union with Christ.*
Christ the Son	*He is our salvation, and all the benefits of salvation flow from him.*

4.4. Grammar Focus: Discourse Connectors

Activity

Ordering	*At first, First, Second*
Summary	*In conclusion*
Addition	*Furthermore, Even more*
Exemplification and restatement	*That is, For instance, Specifically*
Result	*Therefore, Thus, Accordingly*
Concession	*Nevertheless, Nonetheless*
Contrast	*However, In contrast, Conversely, Yet, Though, But*

4.5. Sin and Salvation (Answers in this section may vary)

After reading, complete Chart 1 below.

Chart 1

Paragraph	Focus: Justification, Sanctification, or Both?	One Important Point from the Paragraph
1	*both*	*Answers may vary*
2	*justification*	*Answers may vary*
3	*sanctification*	*Answers may vary*
4	*both*	*Answers may vary*
5	*both*	*Answers may vary*

Chart 2

List the similarities between justification and sanctification	List the differences between justification and sanctification
Appropriate terms: *effects of sin, salvation, faith, benefits, union with Christ*	*Appropriate terms:* *Justification: guilt, event, righteousness, declaration* *Sanctification: corruption, process, purging, incomplete in this life, good works*

Two Soteriological Dangers

Summarize legalism in one sentence.

> <u>Legalism means to try to be righteous by our own efforts and improvement.</u>

Summarize antinomianism in one sentence.

> <u>We do not believe we need to behave righteously because of Christ's work.</u>

4.6 Knowing the Real God and His Salvation (Answers in this section may vary)

Read the following sentences and decide if they are true (T) or false (F).

(1) God saves us because we are good enough. *F*

(2) Jesus Christ is only an example of how to live rightly. *F*

(3) Good works come before salvation. *F*

(4) If we are united to Christ, then God loves us as he loves Christ. *T*

(5) If we are saved, then it does not matter how we live. *F*

(6) Certain people are so good that they do not need Christ's righteousness. *F*

(7) What saves us is God's own righteousness, the righteousness of Christ. *T*

(8) We can never be sure that we are good enough and so we can never be sure that we are saved. *F*

Reading

Comprehension Questions

(1) What was the main thing that changed Luther's understanding of God?

> <u>He learned to picture God as a loving father.</u>

(2) What did Luther know about God before his discovery?

> <u>He knew that God is righteous and hates sin.</u>

(3) How did Luther feel about God before his discovery?

> <u>Before, he felt disconnected from God. After, he felt that he knew God rightly.</u>

(4) Why did Luther pray to Mary and other saints instead of to God?

> *He prayed to Mary and other saints because he saw them as kinder and more merciful than God.*

(5) Where does the righteousness that God gives us come from?

> *It comes as a gift from God through Jesus Christ.*

(6) Luther said it was not enough to know God only as creator and judge. How does this relate to the previous chapter's discussion of general revelation?

> *We need special revelation to know God as Trinity (as Father, Son, and Spirit) and as savior.*

(7) How did God most fully reveal himself?

> *Through his Son Jesus Christ.*

(8) Why can we *really* love God?

> *We can really love God because he really loves us.*

Chapter 5: Creation

5.1 Introduction: The Triune Creator

Listing in the chart all of the verses in Genesis 1 that have the phrase "God said":

	Verse Numbers
"God said . . ."	3, 6, 9, 11, 14, 20, 24, 26, 28, 29

Based on the reading, decide if the following sentences are true (T) or false (F).

(1) We need to understand the Trinity to understand the divine act of creation. *T*

(2) Each person of the Trinity performs different, but related, actions. *F*

(3) The doctrine of inseparable operations is true for all of God's actions. *T*

(4) John 1 helps us to better understand God's act of creation in Genesis 1. *T*

(5) The Spirit's role in creation is more important than the roles of the Father and the Son. *F*

(6) The Father brings about the effect of the Word that the Spirit speaks. _F_

(7) The persons of the Trinity perform different roles, but not different actions. _T_

5.2 The Creator and His Creatures

Grammar Focus 1: Infinitives and Gerunds (Answers in this section may vary)

(1) One of the most important distinctions in theology is the one that distinguishes the creator from his creation. This is called the creator–creature distinction. God alone is the creator, and all that he has made is his creation. Being created by God, humans are creatures. God exists completely from himself, not needing anything else for his existence. We call this God's aseity. He has complete life in himself. In contrast, humans, like all creatures, rely on God {to exist}. To be a creature is to be completely dependent upon God for your existence. To be a creature is to exist in a relation of complete dependence upon God. Existing in a state of complete dependence upon God is what makes each one of us a creature. Being a creature is relying on God for everything. To be a creature, then, is to receive the gift of existence from God himself.

(2) Therefore, the doctrine of creation begins with the doctrine of God. {To understand} creation, we must understand the creator. Explaining this doctrinal connection, the theologian John Webster writes, "Christian teaching about creation is ordered by confession and acclamation of God's matchless self-sufficiency. In his inner works as Father, Son and Spirit, God is plenitude of life and incomparable excellence." God is matchless in his self-sufficiency because, unlike everything else that exists, he exists completely from himself. Existing in this way also means that God has a plenitude, a complete fullness, of life in himself. Having full joy in the communion of the Father, Son, and Spirit, the triune God creates not {to gain} joy but {to give} it. God creates {to share} with us the fullness of his joyful Triune life. To be a creature, then, is to be made {to share} in God's own plenitude of joy.

(3) The theologian Thomas Weinandy helps us {to see} how important the title of creator is to rightly understand our relation to God. Weinandy writes, "Creator specifies both the relationship between Yahweh and his creation and simultaneously his radical distinctiveness from creation." Having created us from nothing, God has an incomparably close relationship to us. He knows us and acts upon us more directly than even we know and act upon ourselves. Having given all creatures their existence, he has an incomparable closeness, a matchless intimacy, to each of them. God's closeness, his intimacy, to creation

is his immanence. However, the title of creator also communicates the great distinction between God and creation. To speak creation into existence from nothing means that God is completely different from and wholly other than his creation. Theologians call God's act of creating from nothing his creation *ex nihilo*. Only because God is completely different from his creation can he create in this way. The wholly otherness of God is his transcendence. Accordingly, Weinandy shows how God's transcendence (his otherness from us) and his immanence (his closeness to us) work together, rather than against each other. It is because God is wholly other than us that he can be incomparably close to us. It is because he is the transcendent God that he is also the immanent God. As Weinandy writes:

> (4) The Old Testament never conceives of God's transcendence in opposition to his immanence, as if what makes God wholly other is different from that which allows him {to be} a personal God who lovingly acts in time and history . . . For God to be transcendent in the biblical understanding means that he is wholly other than the created order but not apart from the created order. That which makes him divine, and thus wholly other and so transcendent, is that which equally allows him {to be} active within the created order and so be immanent. There is no opposition between God's transcendent being and his immanent activity.

Grammar Focus 2: Infinitives and Gerunds

Completing the paragraph with the infinitive form of the verb, the gerund form of the verb, or both.

The creator–creature distinction intends to distinguish God from everything he has created. When we fail to make this distinction, we insist on rejecting both who God is and who we are. To deny/denying this distinction is a case of committing idolatry. We like to think of/thinking of ourselves as the ones who have aseity. However, the fact that we are dependent upon God for our very existence is a wonderful truth. As John Webster explains, to embrace/embracing this truth is to realize/realizing that God loves to share/sharing his own fullness of joy. The Father, Son, and Spirit eternally enjoy communing with one another, and it is this joy that God intends to lavish upon us as his creatures. Therefore, we must avoid thinking that God created us to gain a joy that he was missing. Instead, the fullness of God's delight in himself is the basis of understanding the doctrine of creation. We can only appreciate existing as wholly dependent upon him when we learn to recognize the fullness of joy he intends <u>to give</u> to us. This is the very purpose for which the Father sent his Son, <u>to save</u> us from our sin and <u>to bring</u> us back into a right relationship with himself. <u>To be/Being</u> united to Christ is <u>to participate/participating</u> in the triune communion of the Father, Son, and Holy Spirit.

5.3 The Goodness of Creation and the Problem of Sin (Answers in this section may vary)

Read again through Genesis 1.
How many times does God describe what he created as good? _7_

Vocabulary List

Chapter 1

Divine (adj.): To be God; of or from God

Doctrine (n.) / Doctrinal (adj.): Synonym for theology; a specific theological topic (e.g. the doctrine of the Trinity)

Eternal (adj.): Outside of time; without beginning or end

Exegesis (n.) / Exegetical (adj.): The practice of reading, interpreting, and understanding biblical texts

Heresy (n.) / Heretical (adj.): Theological beliefs against orthodoxy, especially regarding the main aspects of Christian doctrine

Incarnation (n.): The event of the Son of God becoming human, taking on a fully human nature

Monotheism (n.) / Monotheistic (adj.): The belief that there is only one God

Orthodoxy (n.) / Orthodox (adj.): True theological beliefs, especially regarding the main aspects of Christian doctrine

Polytheism (n.) / Polytheistic (adj.): The belief that there is more than one God

The Trinity (n.) / Trinitarian/Triune (adj.): The Christian God who exists as one God in three persons: the Father, the Son, and the Holy Spirit

Chapter 2

Blasphemy (n.): Speech that attacks God

Christology (n.) / Christological (adj.): The doctrine of Jesus Christ, both who he is (his person) and what he has done (his work)

Hermeneutics (n.) / Hermeneutical (adj.): The study and/or practice of reading and interpreting texts

Incarnation (n.): The event of the Son of God becoming human, taking on a fully human nature

Chapter 3

Biblical theology (noun phrase): A theological method that follows biblical themes in Scripture through the course of redemptive history

Fulfillment (n.) / Fulfill (v.): In the Bible, this speaks of God doing what he promised to do

Illumination (n.) / Illuminate (v.): The process by which the Holy Spirit enables Christians to understand, believe, and love what they read in Scripture

Inerrancy (n.) / Inerrant (adj.): The doctrine that states that Scripture is true and without error in everything it affirms

Inspiration (n.) / Inspire (v.): The process by which the Holy Spirit worked through the human writers of Scripture to produce texts that are authored fully by God and fully by humans

Typology (n.) / Typological (adj.): A hermeneutical practice that interprets Christ as the perfection of important roles and institutions found in the Old Testament

Chapter 4

Atonement (n.) / Atone (v.): Christ's reconciliation of sinners to God which Christ achieves by his completed work

Imputation (n.) / Impute (v.): General use: the act of crediting or transferring something to another person; theological use: the act by which Christ gives us his righteousness

Justification (n.) / Justify (v.): The act of God declaring us righteous because Christ has given us his own righteousness

Reformer (n.): A Protestant church leader during the time of the Reformation

Righteousness (n.) / Righteous (adj.): A right standing or status before God and a right relationship with him

Sanctification (n.) / Sanctify (v.): The process by which the Holy Spirit removes the corruption of sin

Soteriology (n.) / Soteriological (adj.): The doctrine of salvation

Union with Christ (noun phrase): The largest category of our salvation because all of the benefits of salvation come from this personal union; the bond that unites us to Christ through faith by the work of the Holy Spirit

Wrath (n.): God's anger against and punishment of sin

Chapter 5

Aseity (n.): The attribute of God that describes his lack of dependence upon anything else and affirms that he has life wholly in and from himself

The created order (noun phrase): Another way to speak of God's creation

Creation ex nihilo *(noun phrase):* God's act of creation by which he made all things from nothing, from no other pre-existing matter or material (*ex nihilo* is Latin for "from nothing")

The fall (noun phrase): The event in which Adam and Eve disobeyed God in the garden of Eden and allowed sin to enter the world

Immanence (n.) / Immanent (adj.): The attribute of God that describes his closeness and intimacy to creation as its creator

Transcendence (n.) / Transcendent (adj.): The attribute of God that describes his wholly otherness, his complete dissimilarity, from creation as its creator

Langham
PARTNERSHIP

Langham Literature and its imprints are a ministry of Langham Partnership.

Langham Partnership is a global fellowship working in pursuit of the vision God entrusted to its founder John Stott –

> *to facilitate the growth of the church in maturity and Christ-likeness through raising the standards of biblical preaching and teaching.*

Our vision is to see churches in the majority world equipped for mission and growing to maturity in Christ through the ministry of pastors and leaders who believe, teach and live by the Word of God.

Our mission is to strengthen the ministry of the Word of God through:
- nurturing national movements for biblical preaching
- fostering the creation and distribution of evangelical literature
- enhancing evangelical theological education

especially in countries where churches are under-resourced.

Our ministry

Langham Preaching partners with national leaders to nurture indigenous biblical preaching movements for pastors and lay preachers all around the world. With the support of a team of trainers from many countries, a multi-level programme of seminars provides practical training, and is followed by a programme for training local facilitators. Local preachers' groups and national and regional networks ensure continuity and ongoing development, seeking to build vigorous movements committed to Bible exposition.

Langham Literature provides majority world preachers, scholars and seminary libraries with evangelical books and electronic resources through publishing and distribution, grants and discounts. The programme also fosters the creation of indigenous evangelical books in many languages, through writer's grants, strengthening local evangelical publishing houses, and investment in major regional literature projects, such as one volume Bible commentaries like *The Africa Bible Commentary* and *The South Asia Bible Commentary*.

Langham Scholars provides financial support for evangelical doctoral students from the majority world so that, when they return home, they may train pastors and other Christian leaders with sound, biblical and theological teaching. This programme equips those who equip others. Langham Scholars also works in partnership with majority world seminaries in strengthening evangelical theological education. A growing number of Langham Scholars study in high quality doctoral programmes in the majority world itself. As well as teaching the next generation of pastors, graduated Langham Scholars exercise significant influence through their writing and leadership.

To learn more about Langham Partnership and the work we do visit **langham.org**

www.ingramcontent.com/pod-product-compliance
Lightning Source LLC
Chambersburg PA
CBHW060400090426
42734CB00011B/2204